北大版新一代对外汉语教材·汉字教程系列

新编

汉字津梁

施正宇 ◎ 编著

上 第一册

插　图：贾　克
帅　梅
古文缮写：李家通
吴本清
英文翻译：赵　晗

北京大学出版社
PEKING UNIVERSITY PRESS

图书在版编目(CIP)数据

新编汉字津梁. 上/施正宇编著. —北京：北京大学出版社，2005.8
ISBN 978-7-301-09254-5

Ⅰ. 新… Ⅱ. 施… Ⅲ. 汉字–对外汉语教学–教材 Ⅳ. H195.4

中国版本图书馆CIP数据核字(2005)第064981号

书　　　　名：新编汉字津梁·上
著作责任者：施正宇　编著
责 任 编 辑：刘　正　lozei@126.com
标 准 书 号：ISBN 978-7-301-09254-5/H·1511
出 版 发 行：北京大学出版社
地　　　　址：北京市海淀区成府路205号　100871
网　　　　址：http://cbs.pku.edu.cn
电　　　　话：邮购部 62752015　发行部 62750672　编辑部 62753334
电 子 邮 箱：zpup@pup.pku.edu.cn
排　　版　者：清鑫工作室
印　　刷　者：涿州市星河印刷有限公司
经　　销　者：新华书店
787毫米×1092毫米　16开本　18印张　390千字
2005年8月第1版　2019年4月第5次印刷
定　　　　价：54.00元（上册全二册）

未经许可，不得以任何方式复制或抄袭本书之部分或全部内容。
版权所有，侵权必究　举报电话：010-62752024
电子邮箱：fd@pup.pku.edu.cn

前　言

《新编汉字津梁》（上、下）是为初学者编写的一部基础汉字教材，旨在通过对汉字形体的分析和对部首字、常用字形音义的说解，帮助初学者学会认读、书写最常用的汉字约 1200 个，以及由这些汉字组成的常用词约 2200 个；并为汉字、汉语的进一步学习打下基础。

本书依据国家汉办颁布的《汉语水平词汇与汉字等级大纲》为初学者设计课时并安排教学进度。所收汉字的 90% 为该大纲中的甲级字和乙级字，考虑到参构汉字的偏旁与部件，以及近年来出现的新词新语，本书也收入少量丙级字、丁级字以及大纲以外的字。

本书结合对外汉字教学的实际，在总结目前汉字学研究成果的基础上，将笔画分为基本笔画——横、竖、撇、点、捺、提和派生笔画，并以国家语言文字工作委员会和中华人民共和国新闻出版署联合发布的《现代汉字通用字笔顺规范》为准，进行笔画顺序教学；依据汉字的构形理据并参考国家语言文字工作委员会语言文字规范 GF3001–1997《信息处理的 GB3000.1 字符集汉字部件规范》，对汉字进行切分。

本书依据造字理据，将属于同一义类的偏旁组成的字分为一个单元，并对部首字进行讲解。对于不能体现原始造字理据的字，包括简化字，按其组成的部件归类。部分原始造字理据不明的汉字，以及一些不易归类或不能单独使用的汉字，依照其参构的复音词的其他字归类。

本书注重字义与词义的联系，注重将汉字与汉语的语言实际结合起来，在讲解字义的同时，也收入了由该字组成的词。收词时，参考《汉语水平词汇与汉字等级大纲》的词汇等级，以甲级词、乙级词为主。随着近年来社会生活的发展，一些过去不太常用的和近年新出现的词语不断出现在人们的日常生活中，对于这些词，本书酌情予以收入。

每个单元后附有"基础知识"部分，扼要讲解汉字的基本理论、书写规律等，"简繁对照"部分将列出与本单元出现的简化字相对应的繁体字。

从1995年起，北大汉语中心为零起点的留学生开设初级汉字课，至今已经十年有余，这期间，教材从无到有，从油印到正式出版，一路踉跄而行，善意的提醒和不同意见为本书的编写提供了思考问题的多种角度。德高望重的林焘先生在古稀之年拨冗做序，更令我日夜笔耕，不敢懈怠。著名书法家、学者吴本清先生擅长各种书体，他为本书所做的摹写，特别是古文字形，均字从典出，不输历代书家之风骨。我的同事宣雅和李海燕两位老师对本书的修改提出了很好的建议，其中宣雅老师协助修改了上册第四单元，李海燕老师协助修改了上册第五单元。她们的才思为本书增添了许多光彩。北京大学对外汉语教育学院的前辈和同事们多有建议和鼓励，言辞切切，成为我完成本书的动力。十多年前，贾克、帅梅两位青年画家为拙作《汉字的故事》所做简洁、生动的插图，让我始终不忍舍弃，这也是我在《新编汉字津梁》（上、下）中继续采用他们插图的当然理由。至于《汉字的故事》中所无、本书所需部分插图，均由李家通先生绘出。既要贴近古人造字的原始意图，又要与已有插图的风格保持一致，着实让家通先生费了一番心思。2004年，本书和即将付梓的汉字中级读本《秀才识字》（上、下）被列为北京大学教材建设项目，北大教务处、出版社为书稿的出版予以支持。在此，谨对所有关心、帮助此书的前辈同侪深表谢意。

写作过程中，小女阿宽不时厮磨于我的耳鬓双膝，她睁大双眼，不停地读着，问着，试图认识书中的每一个字。一天，她突然问我："妈妈，你在给我做书吗？"是的，本书写给每一位汉字的初学者，以及试图以汉字为桥梁学习汉语、了解中国、认识世界的读者，这其中当然也包括我的女儿。

施正宇
2005年春

目录 Contents

第一册

第一单元　汉字的笔画和笔顺 ………………………………… 1
Unit 1　The Strokes and Stroke Orders

  第一课　汉字的基本笔画 / 3
  Lesson 1　The Basic Strokes of Chinese Characters

  第二课　汉字的派生笔画 / 5
  Lesson 2　Derivative Strokes of Chinese Characters

  第三课　汉字的基本笔顺 / 7
  Lesson 3　The Basic Order of Strokes

  第四课　汉字的书写 / 13
  Lesson 4　Writing Characters

第二单元　人 ………………………………………………… 17
Unit 2　People

  第一课　男人 / 19
  Lesson 1　Man

  第二课　女人 / 26
  Lesson 2　Woman

1

第三课 其他人 / 32
Lesson 3　The Others

基础知识 / 41
Basic Knowledge

　　(一)汉字的部件 / 41
　　(Ⅰ)The Component of Chinese Characters

　　(二)繁体和简体 / 41
　　(Ⅱ)The Classical Characters and the Simplified Characters

第三单元　头 ……………………………………… 43
Unit 3　Head

第一课 头(一) / 45
Lesson 1　Head(Ⅰ)

第二课 头(二) / 51
Lesson 2　Head (Ⅱ)

第三课 头(三) / 58
Lesson 3　Head (Ⅲ)

第四课 言语 / 65
Lesson 4　Speech

基础知识 / 71
Basic Knowledge

　　(一)独体字 / 71
　　(Ⅰ)Single Character

　　(二)简化汉字 / 71
　　(Ⅱ)Simplified Characters

第四单元 手 ··· 73
Unit 4 Hand

第一课 手 / 75
Lesson 1　Hand

第二课 又 / 81
Lesson 2　The 又 Radical

第三课 寸和爪 / 88
Lesson 3　The 寸 and 爪 Radical

基础知识 汉字的书写规律·竖钩的变化 / 94
Basic Knowledge Conventions of Writing Chinese Characters·Variations of the Vertical Stroke Ending with a Rising Hook

第五单元 身心 ··· 95
Unit 5　Body and Heart

第一课 身体和病痛 / 97
Lesson 1　Body and Sick

第二课 心（一）/ 102
Lesson 2　Heart（Ⅰ）

第三课 心（二）/ 107
Lesson 3　Heart（Ⅱ）

第四课 心（三）/ 112
Lesson 4　Heart（Ⅲ）

基础知识 汉字的造字方法·象形 / 116
Basic Knowledge Ways How Characters Were Created·Hieroglyphic Characters

第六单元　足 ·· 119
Unit 6　Foot

　　第一课　止 / 121
　　Lesson 1　Toes

　　第二课　辶 / 127
　　Lesson 2　The 辶 Radical

　　第三课　足 / 132
　　Lesson 3　Foot

　　基础知识　汉字的造字方法·指事 / 138
　　Basic Knowledge　Ways How Characters Were Created·Self-explanatory Characters

第二册

第七单元　肉(月)和饮食 ·································· 141
Unit 7　Meat and Cuisine

　　第一课　肉(一) / 143
　　Lesson 1　Meat (Ⅰ)

　　第二课　肉(二) / 148
　　Lesson 2　Meat (Ⅱ)

　　第三课　食品 / 153
　　Lesson 3　Food

　　第四课　米 / 158
　　Lesson 4　Rice

　　基础知识　合体字 / 163
　　Basic Knowledge　Compound Characters

第八单元　动物 ·· 165
Unit 8　Animals

　　　　　第一课　牛、马和鱼 / 167
　　　　　Lesson 1　Ox, Horse and Fish

　　　　　第二课　羊、虫和蛇 / 173
　　　　　Lesson 2　Sheep, Insect and Snake

　　　　　第三课　象、犬和龙 / 179
　　　　　Lesson 3　Elephant, Dog and Dragon

　　　　　第四课　毛、鸟和虎 / 186
　　　　　Lesson 4　Hair, Bird and Tiger

　　　　　第五课　贝 / 194
　　　　　Lesson 5　Shell

　　　　　基础知识　汉字的书写规律·横的变化 / 198
　　　　　Basic Knowledge　Conventions of Writing Chinese Characters·Variations of the Horizontal Stroke

第九单元　植物 ·· 201
Unit 9　Plants

　　　　　第一课　木(一) / 203
　　　　　Lesson 1　Wood(Ⅰ)

　　　　　第二课　木(二) / 210
　　　　　Lesson 2　Wood(Ⅱ)

　　　　　第三课　木(三) / 216
　　　　　Lesson 3　Wood(Ⅲ)

　　　　　第四课　草 / 222
　　　　　Lesson 4　Grass

第五课 竹子 / 228
Lesson 5 Bamboo

第六课 粮食作物及其他 / 235
Lesson 6 Grain Crop and the Others

基础知识 汉字的书写规律·捺笔的变化 / 242
Basic Knowledge Conventions of Writing Chinese Characters·Variation of the Right Downward Stroke

汉字索引 ··· 244
Chinese Character Index

词汇索引 ··· 255
Vocabulary Index

第一单元 汉字的笔画和笔顺
Unit 1 The Strokes and Stroke Orders

第一课　汉字的基本笔画
Lesson 1　The Basic Strokes of Chinese Characters

笔画是构成汉字形体的最小单位，例如，"人"是由撇和捺两个笔画构成的；"十"是由"一"和"丨"构成的。组成汉字的基本笔画有六种，即横、竖、撇、捺、点和提，其余二十多种笔画都是由这六种基本笔画变化而来的。

The stroke is the basic unit to construct characters. For example, the character "人" is made of "丿" and "㇏"; "十" is made of "一" and "丨". There are six basic strokes, and more than 20 others are derived from these six.

横 héng

竖 shù

撇 piě

捺 nà

左点 zuǒdiǎn

右点 yòudiǎn

提 tí

第二课　汉字的派生笔画
Lesson 2　Derivative Strokes of Chinese Characters

横折 héngzhé

竖折 shùzhé

横钩 hénggōu

竖钩 shùgōu

斜钩 xiégōu

弯钩 wāngōu

横折钩 héngzhégōu

竖弯 shùwān

竖弯钩 shùwāngōu

横折弯钩 héngzhéwāngōu

横折弯钩 héngzhéwāngōu

横折弯钩 héngzhéwāngōu

撇折折撇 piězhézhépiě

第三课　汉字的基本笔顺
Lesson 3　The Basic Order of Strokes

书写汉字时笔画出现的先后顺序，叫笔画顺序，简称笔顺。按照合理的笔顺书写汉字，不仅能提高书写的速度，而且能使写出来的汉字美观大方。

The order that rules the writing of a character is called "the order of strokes", sometimes abbreviated into "bishun". It not only facilitates the writing if you use the reasonable orders, but adds to the elegance of the character.

先横后竖"Heng" precedes "shu"

十	一 十		
十	shí	（数）	ten
十一	shíyī	（数）	eleven

干	一 二 干		
干	gàn	（动）	do

七	一 七		
七	qī	（数）	seven

十七	shíqī	（数）	seventeen
七十	qīshí	（数）	seventy

先撇后捺 "Pie" precedes "na"

人 |人| 丿 人

人	rén	（名）	person

八 |八| 丿 八

八	bā	（数）	eight
十八	shíbā	（数）	eighteen
八十	bāshí	（数）	eighty

先上后下 From top to bottom

二 |二| 一 二

二	èr	（数）	two
十二	shí'èr	（数）	twelve
二十	èrshí	（数）	twenty

三 |三| 一 二 三

三	sān	（数）	three
十三	shísān	（数）	thirteen
三十	sānshí	（数）	thirty

第一单元 汉字的笔画和笔顺

工人　　gōngrén　　（名）　　worker

千　　qiān　　（数）　　thousand

个　　gè　　（量）　　a measure word

先左后右 From left to right

儿　　ér　　（名）　　child

几　　jǐ　　（代）　　how many

心　　xīn　　（名）　　heart

先中间后两边 Middle precedes the two sides

9

小	xiǎo	（形）	small；little

山 | 山 山

| 山 | shān | （名） | mountain |

九 | 丿 九

九	jiǔ	（数）	nine
十九	shíjiǔ	（数）	nineteen
九十	jiǔshí	（数）	ninety

先外后里 From the outside to the inside

月 | 丿 几 月 月

月	yuè	（名）	moon；month
一月	yīyuè	（名）	January
二月	èryuè	（名）	February
三月	sānyuè	（名）	March
七月	qīyuè	（名）	July
八月	bāyuè	（名）	August
九月	jiǔyuè	（名）	September
十月	shíyuè	（名）	October
十一月	shíyīyuè	（名）	November
十二月	shí'èryuè	（名）	December

风 | 丿 几 凡 风

风　　　　fēng　　　　（名）　　wind

先填中后封口 The inside precedes the sealing strokes

日　　　　rì　　　　（名）　　day

四　　　　sì　　　　（数）　　four
十四　　　shísì　　　（数）　　fourteen
四十　　　sìshí　　　（数）　　forty
四月　　　sìyuè　　　（名）　　April

练习
Exercises

一、连连看 (Link the characters and the *Pinyin*)：

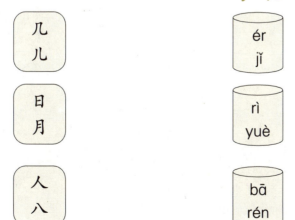

二、按照笔画由少到多排列下面的汉字(Re-match the characters according to their amount of strokes)

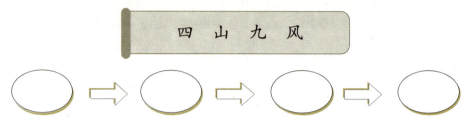

第四课　汉字的书写
Lesson 4　Writing Characters

除了"一""二""三""十"等少数字外，一般情况下，一个汉字的书写，往往需要将两种或两种以上的笔顺规则连续运用才能完成。例如：

Except for a few numerals such as "一"、"二"、"三"and "十", the writing of a character normally requires the combination of two or more rules of orders to complete. For instance：

五	wǔ	（数）	five
十五	shíwǔ	（数）	fifteen
五十	wǔshí	（数）	fifty
五月	wǔyuè	（名）	May
上	shàng	（名）	upward direction
下	xià	（名）	downward direction

| 上午 | shàngwǔ | （名） | morning |
| 下午 | xiàwǔ | （名） | afternoon |

六　　丶一ナ六

六	liù	（数）	six
十六	shíliù	（数）	sixteen
六十	liùshí	（数）	sixty
六月	liùyuè	（名）	June

门　　丶冂门

| 门 | mén | （名） | door |

不　　一ア不不

| 不 | bù | （副） | no; not |

少　　丨丿小少

| 少 | shǎo | （形） | few; little |

两　　一ㄧ丌丙丙两两

| 两 | liǎng | （数） | two |

练习
Exercises

一、连连看 (Link the characters and the *Pinyin*)：

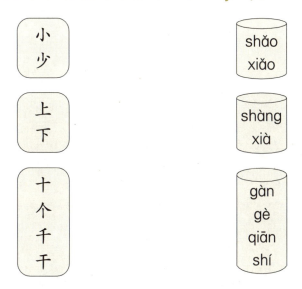

二、按照笔画由少到多排列下面的汉字 (Re-match the characters according to their amount of strokes)

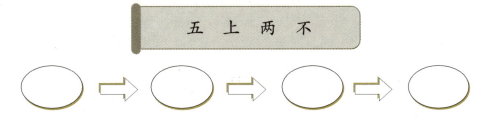

简繁对照

Comparison of Simplified Characters and Classical Characters

儿—兒　　　风—風　　　个—個

几—幾　　　两—兩　　　门—門

第二单元 人
Unit 2 People

第一课 男人
Lesson 1 Man

汉字的派生笔画
Derivative Strokes of Chinese Characters

撇折 piězhé

横折弯钩 héngzhéwāngōu

汉字和汉语词汇
Chinese Characters and Words

人（1）Man

| 我 | 一 二 于 寺 我 我 我 |
| 们 | 丿 亻 亻 仃 们 |

| 我 | wǒ | （代） | I; me |
| 我们 | wǒmen | （代） | we |

大 Big

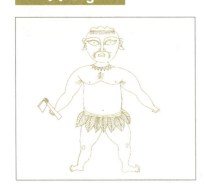

直立着的人，两手两腿张开。

A standing person with arms and legs stretched.

大	一 ナ 大

大	dà	（形）	big; large
大人	dàrén	（名）	adult
大小	dàxiǎo	（名）	size

太	一 ナ 大 太

| 太 | tài | （副） | too |
| 太太 | tàitai | （名） | Mrs.; madam; wife |

夫 Man

束发加簪，以示成年。

Using a stick to do one's hair up, showing adulthood.

第二单元 人

夫　一 二 夫 夫

丈夫	zhàngfu	(名)	husband
大夫	dàifu	(名)	doctor
夫人	fūrén	(名)	lady; madame

• 丈　一 ナ 丈

天　一 二 于 天

天	tiān	(名)	day; the sky
半天	bàntiān	(名)	half a day; a long time
今天	jīntiān	(名)	today

• 半　、 ′ ﹀ 二 半 半

• 今　丿 人 人 今

交 Cross

"大"的两腿交叉在一起。
"大" crosses its legs.

交　、 一 六 六 亣 交

| 交 | jiāo | (动) | to pay; to hand in |

人 People

中国人的祖先是根据直立着的男性的侧面形象来构造"人"这个字的。"人"用作偏旁,常写作"亻",叫单人旁或单立人,表示人,有时也专指男性,也可以表示与人有关的事物或活动。

The ancestors of the Chinese people constructed the word "人" according to the image of the profile of a standing man.

Using "人" as a component, you can write it as "亻", called "the single person component", meaning a person and something exclusively meaning men. It can also be used to indicate things related to human-being's activities.

| 你 | nǐ | (代) | you |
| 你们 | nǐmen | (代) | you |

| 他 | tā | (代) | he; him |
| 他们 | tāmen | (代) | they; them |

位

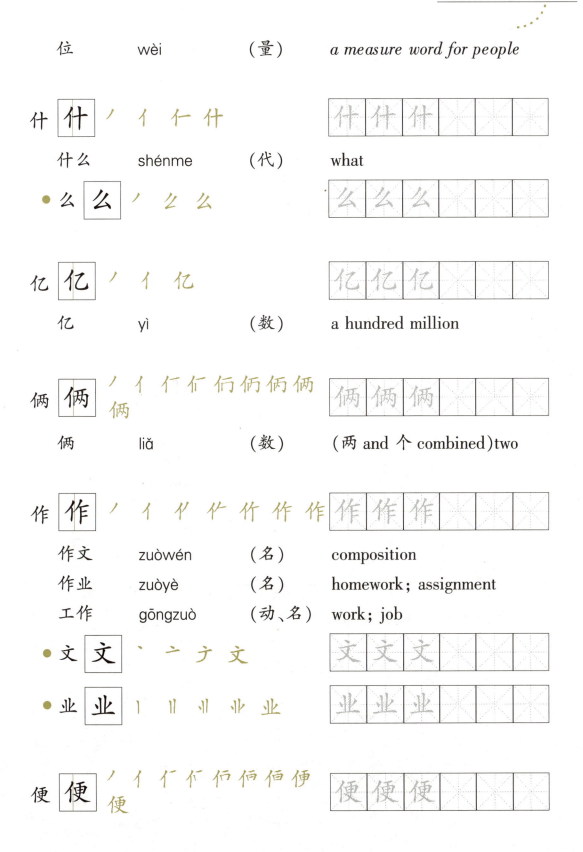

方便　　fāngbiàn　　（形）　　convenient

方 | 方 　 丶 一 方 方

| 方 | 方 | 方 | | |

练习
Exercises

一、连连看 (Link the characters and the *Pinyin*)：

夫　　　　　　bàn
天　　　　　　fū
半　　　　　　tiān

大　　　　　　jiāo
丈　　　　　　wén
文　　　　　　dà
交　　　　　　zhàng

二、按照笔画由少到多排列下面的汉字 (Re-match the characters according to their amount of strokes)：

我　交　他　亿　俩　今

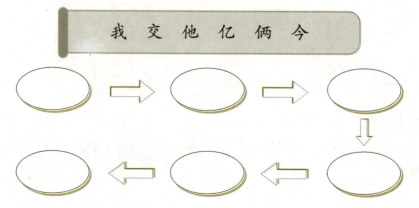

三、用所给汉字组成词语(Form words with the given characters)：

夫：_____ _____ _____

作：_____ _____ _____

第二课 女人
Lesson 2　Woman

汉字的派生笔画
Derivative Strokes of Chinese Characters

撇点 piědiǎn

竖折折钩 shùzhézhégōu

横折折折钩 héngzhézhézhégōu

汉字和汉语词汇
Chinese Characters and Words

女 Woman

"女"的古文字形象两腿跪着，两手相交，是一个被抢来的女子的形象。

现代汉字里，"女"可以单独成字，也可以用作偏旁，写在字的左边，叫女字旁，或在字的下边，表示各种女性，以及和女性有关的事物。

The ancient character "女" resembles image of a kidnapped woman on her knees with hands crossed.

In modern characters, "女" can both be a single character and a radical. Put on the left, called "the woman radical", or put underneath other characters, indicating things related to woman.

女				
女	nǚ	（形）	female
女儿	nǚ'ér	（名）	daughter
女人	nǚrén	（名）	woman

她				
她	tā	（代）	she; her
她们	tāmen	（代）	they; them

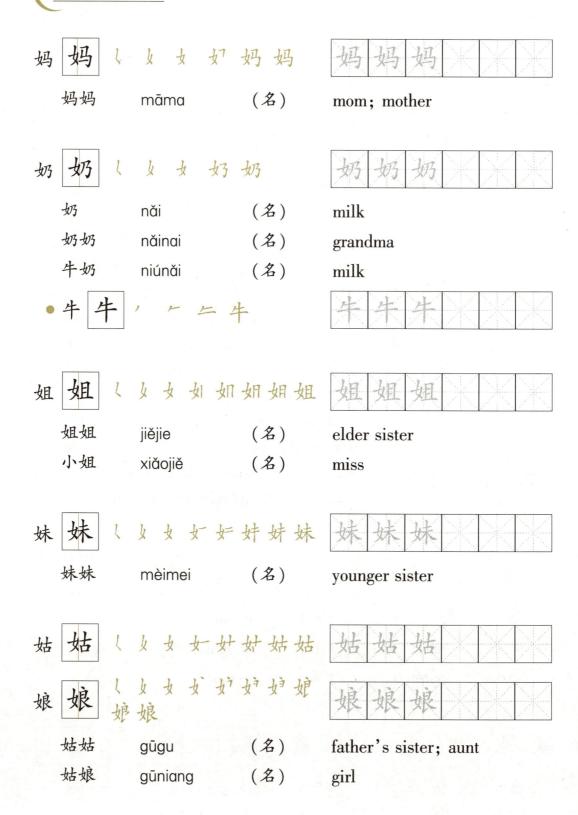

妈妈	māma （名）	mom; mother

奶	nǎi （名）	milk
奶奶	nǎinai （名）	grandma
牛奶	niúnǎi （名）	milk

姐姐	jiějie （名）	elder sister
小姐	xiǎojiě （名）	miss

妹妹	mèimei （名）	younger sister

姑姑	gūgu （名）	father's sister; aunt
姑娘	gūniang （名）	girl

要 要

要　　　yào　　　（助动、动）　　do; want
不要　　búyào　　（副）　　　　do not
重要　　zhòngyào　（形）　　　　important

● 重 重

母 Mother

女性的两个乳房，像哺育过婴儿的妇女形象。

The breasts of a woman indicate that she has fed her baby.

母 母

母亲　　mǔqīn　　（名）　　mother

● 亲 亲 ヽ 亠 亠 产 立 立 辛 辛 亲 | 亲 亲 亲

每 每 ノ 亠 仁 与 每 每 每 | 每 每 每

每　　měi　　（代）　　every; each

29

> 练习
> Exercises

一、请指出下列形符的名称和意义 (Please link the name and meaning of the given radical)：

亻   女字旁

女   单立人

二、按照笔画由少到多排列下面的汉字 (Re-match the characters according to their amount of strokes)：

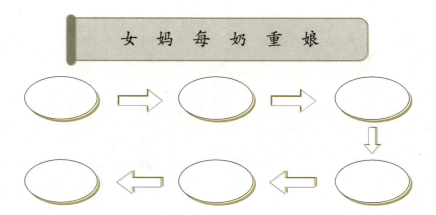

女 妈 每 奶 重 娘

三、用所给汉字组成词语(Form words with the given characters)：

女：_____ _____

奶：_____ _____

姐：_____ _____

要：_____ _____

四、请指出下列每组汉字中共有的部件 (Please write down the common component in the following characters)：

你 他：_____   他 她：_____

姐 妹：_____   什 姑：_____

五、选词填空(Fill in the blanks with the appropriate words)：

1. A：她是你的_____吗？

    B：是的，她是我的_____。

    a. 大大   b. 太太

2. A：_____是你的姐姐吗？

    B：是的，_____是我的姐姐。

    a. 她   b. 他

3. 今天上_____你_____什么？

    a.千   b.午   c.牛   d.干

第三课 其他人
Lesson 3   The Others

汉字的派生笔画
Derivative Strokes of Chinese Characters

竖提 shùtí

横撇 héngpiě

汉字和汉语词汇
Chinese Characters and Words

从 Follow

古文字形象一个人跟着一个人，写作"从"。繁体为"從"，简化字又作"从"。

A person follows another：从. The classical version is "從", the simplified version is "从".

从　　　cóng　　　（介）　　　from

北 North

背靠背的两个人。
Two persons back to back.

| 北 | 北 | 丨 丿 ナ 才 北 | 北 北 北 | | | |

北	běi	（名）	north
北方	běifāng	（名）	north; northern part of the country
北方人	běifāngrén	（名）	northerner
北京	Běijīng	（名）	Beijing

• 京 京 丶 亠 亠 亡 亨 京 京   京 京 京

| 比 | 比 | 一 ト ᅡ 比 | 比 比 比 | | | |

| 比 | bǐ | （介、动） | than(*prep.*); to compare |

| 毕 | 毕 | 一 ト ᅡ 比 毕 毕 | 毕 毕 毕 | | | |

| 毕业 | bì yè | | to graduate |

耂 The Old

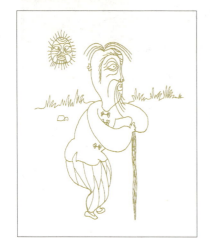

古文字形象拄着拐杖的长发老人。用作偏旁，写在字的上边，作"耂"，叫老字头。

The ancient character resembles a long-haired old man with a crutch in Chinese. As a component, it's written as "耂", call the head of the old.

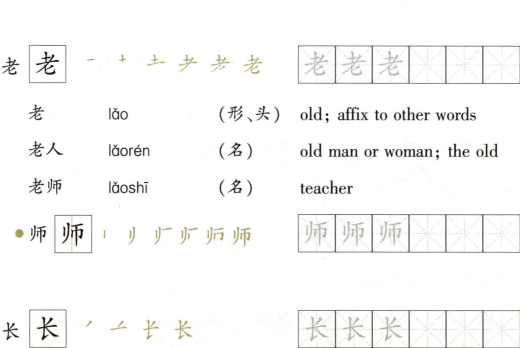

老	一 十 土 耂 耂 老

老	lǎo	（形、头）	old; affix to other words
老人	lǎorén	（名）	old man or woman; the old
老师	lǎoshī	（名）	teacher

• 师　丿 丿 丿 㐃 师 师

| 师 | | | |

| 长 | ノ 一 匕 长 |

| 长 | zhǎng | （动） | to grow |
| 长 | cháng | （形） | long; lengthy |

父 Father

古文字形象手拿石斧。在古代，手里拿石斧干活的多为男子，所以又作父亲的"父"。

现代汉字中，"父"还可以用作偏旁，写在字的上边，表示家中年长的男性。

The ancient character resembles a hand holding an axe. In ancient times, it was mostly men who worked with an axe, and so comes the character for "father".

In modern characters, "父" can be used as a component, usually put on top of other characters, indicating elderly members of the family.

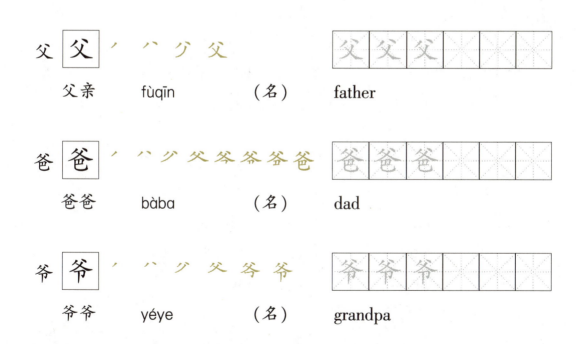

父　父亲　fùqīn　（名）　father

爸　爸爸　bàba　（名）　dad

爷　爷爷　yéye　（名）　grandpa

子 Son

象襁褓中的婴儿,"子"的本义是"幼小的儿女"的意思。现在专指儿子。现代汉字中,子可以用作偏旁,写在字的左边或下边,表示年幼的人。写在字的右边,有时表示这个字的读音。

It looks like a baby in swathes. Its original meaning was "small children", and now that's narrowed down to mean only "son". In modern characters, "子" can be used as a radical, put either on the left, or on the right to indicate the pronunciation.

子 | 子 | 乛 了 子

儿子	érzi	(名)	son
个子	gèzi	(名)	height; stature
日子	rìzi	(名)	days

孩 | 孩 | 乛 了 孑 孑 孑 孑 孩 孩 孩

孩子	háizi	(名)	children
女孩儿	nǚháir	(名)	girl; daughter
小孩儿	xiǎoháir	(名)	kid

孙 | 孙 | 乛 了 孑 孕 孕 孙

| 孙子 | sūnzi | (名) | grandson |
| 孙女 | sūnnǚ | (名) | granddaughter |

好 Good

妈妈和自己的孩子在一起。

It feels good when a mother gets together with her son.

好 好 好 好 好 好

好	ㄑ 乊 女 女 奵 好

好　　hǎo　　　　（形）　　good
你好　　nǐ hǎo　　　　　　hello; how are you; how do you do
好久　　hǎojiǔ　　（名）　a long time

久	ノ 夂 久

学	丶 ⺍ ⺌ ⺍ ⺧ 学 学

学　　　　xué　　　　　　（动）　　to study
上学　　　shàng xué　　　　　　　to go to school
学习　　　xuéxí　　　　　（动、名）to study; the results of studies
学生　　　xuésheng　　　　（名）　student
大学　　　dàxué　　　　　（名）　university
大学生　　dàxuéshēng　　　（名）　university student; collage student
文学　　　wénxué　　　　　（名）　literature
小学　　　xiǎoxué　　　　　（名）　primary school; elementary school
小学生　　xiǎoxuéshēng　　（名）　pupil

留学生　　liúxuéshēng　　（名）　　student studying abroad

- 习　⃞习　㇆ 刁 习
- 生　⃞生　丿 ㇒ ⼆ 牛 生
- 留　⃞留　⺈ ⺈ 丘 丘 𠃌 留 留 留 留

包　A Baby in Uterus

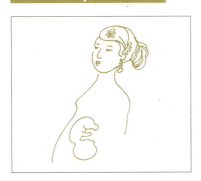

"包"象尚在母体中的婴儿。用作偏旁，省写作"⺈"，叫作包字头。

It resembles a baby still in uterus. When used as a component, the uterus is written as "⺈", called "the head of 包".

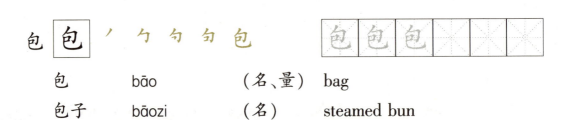

包　⃞包　丿 ⺈ 勹 匀 包

包　　bāo　　（名、量）　bag
包子　bāozi　（名）　　steamed bun

书　⃞书　㇆ ㇇ 书 书

书　　shū　　　（名）　book
书包　shūbāo　（名）　schoolbag; satchel

练习
Exercises

一、请指出下列形符的名称和意义：(Please link the name and meaning of the giver radiced:)

屮　　　包字头

勹　　　老字头

二、按照笔画由少到多排列下面的汉字(Re-match the characters according to their amount of strokes)

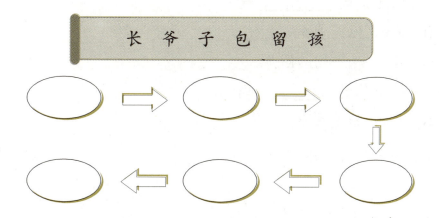

长　爷　子　包　留　孩

三、用所给汉字组成词语(Form words with the given characters)：

北：_____ _____ _____

子：_____ _____ _____

学：_____ _____ _____

人：_____ _____ _____

四、请指出下列每组汉字中共有的部件 (Please write down the common component in the following characters)：

你 京：_____   北 比：_____

爸 爷：_____   老 考：_____

什 毕：_____   好 学：_____

五、选词填空 (Fill in the blanks with the appropriate words)：

1. 我的爷爷是一位_____。
   a. 大天   b. 太夫   c. 大夫   d. 太天

2. A：_____是你的父亲吗?
   B：是的，_____是我的父亲。
   a. 她   b. 他

3. A：他是你的_____吗?
   B：是的，他是我的_____。
   a. 孙子   b. 孙女

4. A：她是你的_____吗?
   B：是的，她是我的_____。
   a. 儿子   b. 女儿

基础知识
Basic Knowledge

（一）汉字的部件
(Ⅰ) The Component of Chinese Characters

组成汉字的最小的笔画结构单位叫部件。

The smallest stroke-group in forming a character is a component.

（二）繁体和简体
(Ⅱ) The Classical Characters and the Simplified Characters

繁体和简体是相对而言的，简体是繁体的简化写法，笔画比繁体少。

汉字是从图画文字发展而来的，从不同的角度结构的形体，汉字自古以来就存在着繁体和简体两种形式。封建社会中，繁体字为正字，简体字一直在民间流传、使用，被视为俗体，不能登大雅之堂。进入20世纪，伴随着科学、民主呼声的日益高涨，为扫除文盲、普及教育，一些仁人志士提出了采用简体字的主张，1949年中华人民共和国成立之前，简体字运动已经得到了蓬勃发展。

The simplified characters are taken from the classical characters. When a character has got two or more versions, the version(s) with the more strokes are called "the classical versions", and that with the fewer strokes are called "the simplified version".

The Chinese characters originated with picture. Structured from different perspectives, the characters have had these versions since old times. In the feudal society, the classical characters were used in the formal (official) language, and the simplified version were used by the common people in the "vulgar" day-to-day speeches and couldn't be used officially. At the beginning of the 20th century, with the rising calls for science and democracy , some people advocated the use of simplified characters in a bid to make it easier for the elimination of illiteracy and for the spread of education. By 1949, when the People's Republic of China founded, the move to popularize simplified characters had already been thriving.

简繁对照
Comparison of Simplified Characters and Classical Characters

俩—倆	亿—億	业—業	从—從
毕—畢	师—師	长—長	亲—親
爷—爺	妈—媽	孙—孫	学—學
习—習	书—書		

第三单元 头

Unit 3 Head

第一课 头（一）
Lesson 1　Head（Ⅰ）

汉字和汉语词汇
Chinese Characters and Words

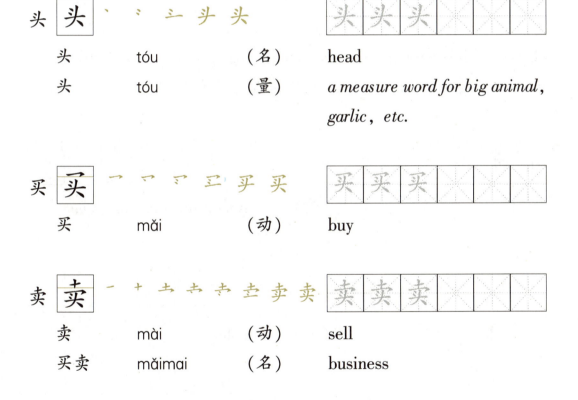

头	tóu	（名）	head
头	tóu	（量）	a measure word for big animal, garlic, etc.
买	mǎi	（动）	buy
卖	mài	（动）	sell
买卖	mǎimai	（名）	business

页 Head/Page

古文字形突出了人的头部。现代汉字中,"页"用作偏旁,仍可表示与头有关的事物,一般多写在字的右边;单独成字时,"页"可用作表示纸张的量词,已不表示"头"的意思。字形繁体作"頁"。

The ancient character "页" emphasized the head of a person. when used as a part, "页" can still form words related with a person's head, usually as a right part. When used as a character, it has the meaning of a measuring word for paper, but not the meaning of head. The classical version is "頁".

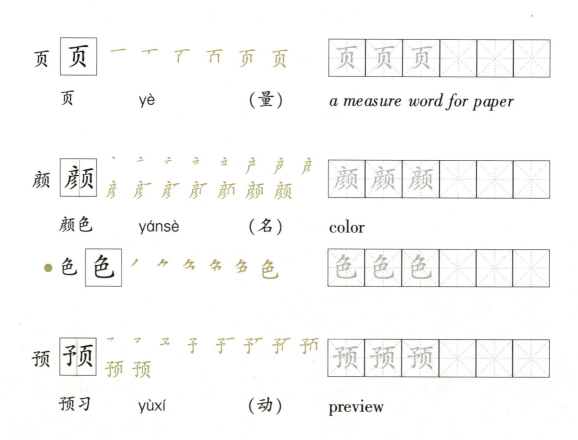

页　页　一 丆 厂 厅 页 页　　页 页 页
页　　yè　　（量）　a measure word for paper

颜　彦　丶 亠 亣 立 产 产 彦
　　　彦 彦 彦 彦 颜 颜 颜　　颜 颜 颜
颜色　yánsè　（名）　color

• 色　色　ノ 冖 ⺈ 夆 夆 色　　色 色 色

预　予　フ 丆 乛 予 予 予 矛 预
　　　预 预　　　　　　　　预 预 预
预习　yùxí　（动）　preview

首 Head

"首"的古文字形,象头的形状。

The ancient character resembles a head.

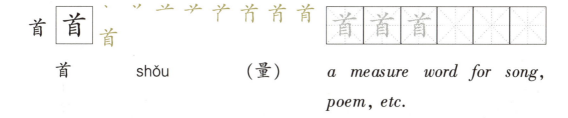

首 | 首 | 丶 丷 尣 产 产 首 首 首

首　shǒu　（量）　*a measure word for song, poem, etc.*

目 Eye

古文字形象人的眼睛。用作偏旁,写在字的左边、右边或下边,多表示与眼睛的部位、动作有关的事物。

The ancient character resembles eyes in Chinese. It is usually used as a radical a character's left, right or underneath, indicating the place and action of the eyes.

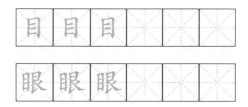

目 | 丨 冂 冃 冃 目

眼 | 丨 冂 冃 冃 目 目' 目' 目' 胆 眼 眼

睛 丨 冂 冃 月 目 目ˊ 目ˊ 目±
睛 睁 睁 睛 睛 睛

眼睛　　yǎnjing　　（名）　　eye

眉 ⁻ ⁼ ⁼ ⁼ 尸 尸 尸 眉 眉
眉

眉毛　　méimao　　（名）　　eyebrow

• 毛　ˊ ⁼ 三 毛

睡 丨 冂 冃 月 目 目ˊ 目ˊ 目±
睡 睁 睁 睡 睡

睡觉　　shuì jiào　　　　　　sleep

• 觉 ˋ ˊ ˊ ˇ ⁺ ⁺ 学 学
觉 觉

面 ⁻ ⁻ ⁻ 厂 丆 而 而 面
面

面包　　miànbāo　　（名）　　bread
北面　　běimiàn　　（名）　　north
上面　　shàngmiàn　（名）　　the up direction
下面　　xiàmiàn　　（名）　　the downward direction

民 ⁻ ⁻ ⁻ 尸 民 民

人民　　rénmín　　　（名）　　people
人民币　rénmínbì　　（名）　　RMB

 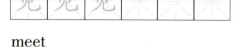

见面　　jiàn miàn　　　　meet
再见　　zàijiàn　　（动）　goodbye

练习
Exercises

一、按照笔画由少到多排列下面的汉字(Re-match the characters according to their amount of strokes)：

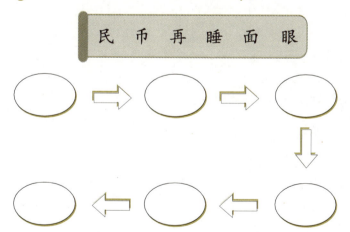

二、用所给汉字组成词语(Form words with the given characters)：

面：_____　_____

见：_____　_____

三、请指出下列每组汉字中共有的部件(Please write down the common component in the following characters)：

学 觉：_____　　　预 颜：_____

眼 睡：_____

第二课 头（二）
Lesson 2　Head（Ⅱ）

汉字和汉语词汇
Chinese Characters and Words

口　Mouth

古文字形象人张开的嘴。用作偏旁,多写在字的左边,叫口字旁,也可以写在其他位置上,表示与口的部位、动作有关的事物。不过,由于长时期的发展与演变,由"口"组成的汉字,已不都表示与嘴有关的事物了。

The ancient character resembles an open mouth. When used as left radical, called "口"radical. "口"radical also appears in other parts of a character. Usually it forms words related with a mouth's place and action, yet not always so, due to the long history of the Chinese language's development and alteration.

口　囗　丨　冂　口

口	kǒu	（名、量）	mouth
人口	rénkǒu	（名）	population
入口	rùkǒu	（名）	entrance

• 入 入　丿 入

只 只　丶 冂 冂 尸 只

只　　　zhī　　　（量）　a measure word for animal, etc.

中 中　丨 冂 口 中

中　　　zhōng　　（名、形）　middle
中文　　Zhōngwén　（名）　　Chinese
中午　　zhōngwǔ　　（名）　　noon
中心　　zhōngxīn　　（名）　　center
中学　　zhōngxué　　（名）　　high school

站 站　丶 亠 亠 亣 立 刬 並 站 站 站

站　　　zhàn　　（动）　stand
站　　　zhàn　　（名）　station

古 古　一 十 十 古 古

古代　　gǔdài　　（名）　ancient time

• 代 代　丿 亻 仁 代 代

号 号　丶 冂 口 号 号

号　　　hào　　（名）　number; date

第三单元 头

后	丿 厂 厂 斤 后 后

后	hòu	（形）	back
后天	hòutiān	（名）	the day after tomorrow
后面	hòumiàn	（名）	back
后代	hòudài	（名）	offspring; descendants

句	丿 勹 勺 句 句

| 句 | jù | （量） | a measure word for sentence |
| 句子 | jùzi | （名） | sentence |

可	一 丁 厅 可 可

| 可以 | kěyǐ | （助动） | may |
| 可以 | kěyǐ | （形） | OK |

• | 以 | ㇀ ㇀ 以 以 |
|---|---|

哥	一 厂 丙 可 叮 哥 哥 哥

| 哥哥 | gēge | （名） | brother |

台	㇒ ㄙ 乍 台 台

| 台 | tái | （量） | a measure word for television, machine, etc. |

53

| 始 | 乀 女 女 如 如 始 始 | 始 始 始 | | |

开始　　kāishǐ　　（动、名）　　begin；begining

• 开　　一 二 于 开　　开 开 开

| 叫 | 丨 口 口 叫 叫 | 叫 叫 叫 | | |

叫　　jiào　　（动）　　let；call

| 吃 | 丨 口 口 叶 吃 吃 | 吃 吃 吃 | | |

吃　　chī　　（动）　　eat
好吃　　hǎochī　　（形）　　delicious

| 喝 | 丨 口 口 口' 口日 呵 呵 | 喝 喝 喝 | | |
喝 喝 喝 喝

喝　　hē　　（动）　　drink
好喝　　hǎohē　　（形）　　be pleasant to drink

| 喂 | 丨 口 口 口' 口田 哩 喂 | 喂 喂 喂 | | |
喂 喂 喂 喂

喂　　wèi　　（叹）　　Hello
喂　　wèi　　（动）　　feed

| 喊 | 丨 口 口 口' 吁 吁 咸 | 喊 喊 喊 | | |
咸 喊 喊 喊

喊　　hǎn　　（动）　　shout
喊叫　　hǎnjiào　　（动）　　shout；cry out

大喊大叫 dà hǎn dà jiào shout at the top of one's voice

吗 吗 丨 ㄇ 口 口⁷ 吗 吗 吗 吗 吗

吗 ma （助） to express doubt; to ask

吧 吧 丨 ㄇ 口 口⁷ 口⁷ 口⁷ 吧 吧 吧 吧

吧 ba （助） auxiliary word; to show uncertainty

呢 呢 丨 ㄇ 口 口⁷ 口⁷ 口尸 口尸 呢 呢 呢 呢

呢 ne （助） to express doubt or praise

练习
Exercises

一、连连看(Link the characters and the *Pinyin*)：

人 入 八	rén bā rù
只 古 号 后 句 可	hòu jù kě zhī gǔ hào

二、按照笔画由少到多排列下面的汉字(Re-match the characters according to their amount of strokes)

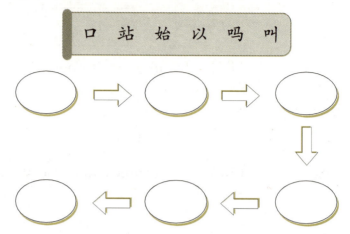

口　站　始　以　吗　叫

三、用所给汉字组成词语(Form words with the given characters)：

中：_____　　_____

口：_____　　_____

后：_____　　_____

四、请指出下列每组汉字中共有的部件 (Please write down the common component in the following characters)：

古 毕：_____　　吧 爸：_____

他 代：_____　　吗 妈：_____

五、选词填空(Fill in the blanks with the appropriate words)：

1. 你_____什么名字(míngzi, name)?

　a. 喊　　b. 叫

2. 面包_____吗？

　a. 好吃　　b. 好喝

3. 你是(shì,are)北京人_____?
   a. 吧   b. 呢   c. 吗   d. 喂

4. 我们吃_____。
   a. 吧   b. 呢   c. 吗   d. 喂

5. 我不是(bú shì,am not)北京人,你_____?
   a. 吧   b. 呢   c. 吗   d. 喂

第三课　头（三）
Lesson 3　Head（Ⅲ）

汉字的派生笔画
Derivative Strokes of Chinese Characters

横折弯 héngzhéwān

汉字和汉语词汇
Chinese Characters and Words

欠 Yawn

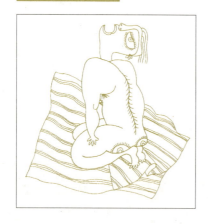

　　古文字形象一个人张着大嘴打哈欠的样子。用作偏旁，表示与呼吸、张嘴有关。

　　The ancient character is like a man yearning, his mouth wide, in ancient Chinese: 欠. When used as a radical, to form words related with breathe and opening one's mouth.

| 吹 | chuī | （动） | blow |
| 吹牛 | chuī niú | | boast |

歌 歌 一 丁 丁 可 可 可 哥 哥 哥 哥 歌 歌 歌　　歌 歌 歌

| 歌 | gē | （名） | song |
| 唱歌 | chànggē | （动） | sing(a song) |

• 唱 唱 丨 冂 冂 叩 叩 呵 唱 唱 唱 唱　　唱 唱 唱

牙 Tooth

"牙"的古文字形象口腔里面两侧的白齿。

The ancient character is like molar teeth in ancient Chinese.

"齿"的古文字形象口中上下交错的牙齿的形象,字形后来加"止(zhǐ)",近似地表示字的读音。字形繁体作"齿"。

People drew teeth in a mouth to express the meaning in ancient Chinese. "止" was later added to give the word its sound. The classical version is "齿".

牙 牙 一 ⼆ 于 牙　　牙 牙 牙

新编汉字津梁

齿 | 齿 | 丨 卜 丨 止 止 牛 齿 齿 | 齿 齿 齿
牙　　yá　　（名）　　tooth
牙齿　yáchǐ　（名）　　tooth

呀 | 呀 | 丨 冂 口 口 吖 吖 呀 呀 | 呀 呀 呀
呀　　ya　　（助）　　oops

自 Nose

古文字形象鼻子的形状。说到自己时，人们常常指着自己的鼻子，所以这个字后来就当"自己"讲。"鼻"是后来产生的字，其中"畀(bì)"近似地表示字的读音。

The ancient character looks like a nose in ancient Chinese. When referring to oneself, people pointed to their own noses. Later "自" started to be referred to as one's self. "鼻" came into being later than"自"，"畀"to lend the words sound.

自 | 自 | ′ ⺈ 冂 白 白 自 | 自 自 自
自己　zìjǐ　（代）　　self

• 己 | 己 | ¬ ⊐ 己 | 己 己 己

咱　咱　丨 ㇇ 口 口' 口ʼ 叼 咱 咱　咱 咱 咱

咱　zán　（代）　we(including both the speaker and the person or persons spoken to)

鼻　鼻　′ ㇒ 丆 自 自 自 畠 鼻　鼻 鼻 鼻
　　　　臬 臬 畠 疊 鼻 鼻

鼻子　bízi　（名）　nose

耳 Ear

古文字形象耳朵的形状。用作偏旁，常写在字的左边，多表示与耳朵及听有关的事物。

The ancient character is like an ear. Often used as a left characters related with ears and hearing.

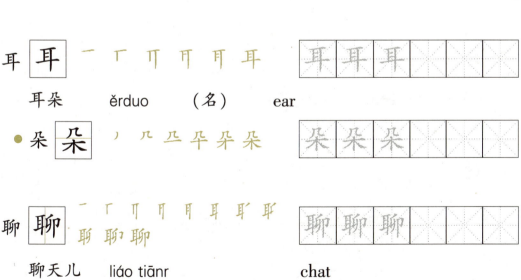

耳　耳　一 丆 丅 圧 耳 耳　耳 耳 耳

耳朵　ěrduo　（名）　ear

• 朵　朵　丿 几 几 朶 朵 朵　朵 朵 朵

聊　聊　一 丆 丅 圧 耳 耳 耶 耶　聊 聊 聊
　　　　耶 聊 聊

聊天儿　liáo tiānr　　chat

职	一 丆 丌 爿 耳 耳 耵 职 职 职					

职业	zhíyè	（名）	occupation
职工	zhígōng	（名）	workers and staff members

听	一 口 口 叮 叽 听 听					

听	tīng	（动）	listen(to)
听见	tīng jiàn		hear
好听	hǎotīng	（形）	sound pleasant

写	丶 冖 冖 写 写					

写	xiě	（动）	write
听写	tīngxiě	（动、名）	dictate; dictation

• 声	一 十 士 吉 吉 声					

音	丶 亠 亣 立 产 音 音 音					

声音	shēngyīn	（名）	sound

章	丶 亠 亣 立 产 音 音 音 音 章 章					

文章	wénzhāng	（名）	article

练习
Exercises

一、看图写字(Write characters according to the picture)：

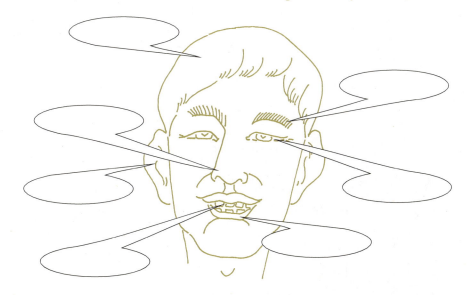

二、按照笔画由少到多排列下面的汉字(Re-match the characters according to their amount of strokes)

牙 耳 声 音 写 鼻

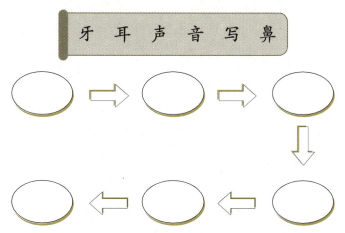

三、用所给汉字组成词语(Form words with the given characters)：

写：_____ _____

听：_____ _____

职：_____ _____

四、请指出下列每组汉字中共有的部件（Please write down the common component in the following characters）：

鼻 咱：_____　　　　声 眉：_____

聊 职：_____　　　　呀 听：_____

五、选词填空(Fill in the blanks with the appropriate words)：

1. 爸爸和奶奶_____天儿呢。

　a. 职　　　b. 聊

2. 妹妹唱_____呢。

　a. 歌　　　b. 哥

3. 你的声_____很好听。

　a. 章　　　b. 音

第四课 言语
Lesson 4　Speech

汉字的派生笔画
Derivative Strokes of Chinese Characters

横折提 héngzhétí

汉字和汉语词汇
Chinese Characters and Words

言 Speech

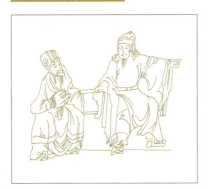

现代汉字中,"言"既可以是从口中说出的话,也可以指"说"的动作。用作偏旁,可写在字的下边或右边;位于字的左边时,"言"简化作"讠",叫言字旁,表示与言语行为有关的事物。

In modern Chinese, "言" refers to both the spoken words and the action of speaking, used as a right part or under part. "言" used as left part has been simplified into "讠", called "the speech radical", to form words related with words and speech.

语

`、讠讠ì讠讠语语语`

| 语言 | yǔyán | (名) | language |
| 口语 | kǒuyǔ | (名) | oral speech |

言

`、亠亠言言言`

信

`丿亻亻亻亻信信信信`

| 信 | xìn | (名) | letter |
| 信 | xìn | (动) | believe; trust |

说

`、讠讠ì ì ì ì 说说`

说	shuō	(动)	say
听说	tīngshuō	(动)	hear
小说	xiǎoshuō	(名)	novel

讲

`、讠讠ì 讲讲`

| 讲 | jiǎng | (动) | speak |
| 听讲 | tīngjiǎng | (动) | listen to (a lecture) |

词

`、讠讠词词词词`

词	cí	(名)	word
生词	shēngcí	(名)	new word
学生	xuésheng	(名)	student

- 生 生 ノ 仁 牛 生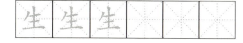

认 认 丶 讠 认 认
识 识 丶 讠 讠 沢 识 识 识

    认识   rènshi   （动）   know; knowledge
    认真   rènzhēn   （形）   serious

- 真 真 一 十 广 占 占 百 百 直 真 真

读 读 丶 讠 讠 计 读 读 读 读 读

    读   dú   （动）   read
    读书   dú shū   read(a book)

课 课 丶 讠 讠 沢 识 识 评 评 课 课

    课   kè   （名）   lesson
    课文   kèwén   （名）   text
    上课   shàng kè   have class(es)
    下课   xià kè   dismiss a class

让 让 丶 讠 让 让 让

    让   ràng   （动）   let; have

三

记　丶 讠 订 记

| 记 | jì | (动) | memorize; note down |
| 日记 | rìjì | (名) | diary; journal |

论　丶 讠 讠 讫 论

| 论文 | lùnwén | (名) | thesis; paper |

试　丶 讠 讠 讠 讧 试 试

试	shì	(动)	try
考试	kǎoshì	(动、名)	exam; test
口试	kǒushì	(动)	test orally
面试	miànshì	(动)	interview

• 考　一 十 土 耂 考

许　丶 讠 讠 讠 许

允许	yǔnxǔ	(动)	allow; permit
不许	bùxǔ	(动)	forbid
也许	yěxǔ	(副)	perhaps

• 允　亠 厶 夯 允

• 也　𠃍 也 也

谁　丶 讠 讠 讠 讠 诈 诈 谁 谁

| 谁 | shéi | (代) | who |

练习
Exercises

一、请指出下列偏旁的名称和意义（Please point out the name and meaning of the given radical）：

讠   目字旁

口   口字旁

目   言字旁

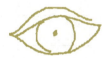

二、连连看(Link the characters and the *Pinyin*)：

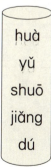

说　　huà
讲　　yǔ
读　　shuō
话　　jiǎng
语　　dú

三、按照笔画由少到多排列下面的汉字(Re-match the characters according to their amount of strokes)

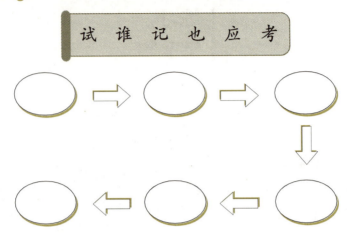

四、用所给汉字组成词语(Form words with the given characters)：

课：_____ _____

许：_____ _____

文：_____ _____

试：_____ _____

说：_____ _____

五、请指出下列每组汉字中共有的部件 (Please write down the common component in the following characters)：

识 职：_____   考 老：_____

语 词：_____   信 作：_____

基础知识
Basic Knowledge

(一) 独体字
(Ⅰ) Single Character

由笔画直接构成的汉字叫独体字。

Characters constructed directly with strokes are called single character.

(二) 简化汉字
(Ⅱ) Simplified Characters

繁体字笔画繁多,不利书写。为了普及教育,提高人民的文化素质,1956年,中国政府公布了《汉字简化方案》。这个方案采用了个体简化和类推简化两种方式,对515个繁体字和54个繁体偏旁进行了简化。1964年,《简化字总表》正式发布。1986年,经过个别调整而重新发表的《简化字总表》共收简化字2235个。这是目前为止经国家批准公布的全部简化汉字。

Classical characters usually have many strokes, which make the characters hard to write. For the sake of spreading education, and improving the quality of people in culture, the Chinese government published in 1956 *The Outline for Simplified Characters*. This outline adopted direct simplification and derivative simplification, and simplified 515 classical characters and 54 radicals. In 1964, *Complete list of*

Simplified Characters was published. The 1986 re-issues of this book listed 2235 simplified characters, which are the entire pool of simplified characters officially approved by the government.

简繁对照
Comparison of Simplified Characters and Classical Characters

头—頭	买—買	卖—賣	号—號
后—後	台—臺	开—開	吗—嗎
见—見	觉—覺	只(zhī)—隻	齿—齒
职—職	听—聽	写—寫	声—聲
页—頁	颜—顏	须—須	预—預
语—語	说—説	讲—講	词—詞
认—認	识—識	读—讀	课—課
让—讓	应—應	该—該	记—記
论—論	试—試	许—許	谁—誰

第四单元 手
Unit 4 Hand

第四单元 手

第一课 手
Lesson 1 Hand

汉字和汉语词汇
Chinese Characters and Words

手 hand

古文字形象一只手五个指头的形状。用作偏旁，可写在字的下边或右边；在字的左边，写作"扌"，叫提手旁，表示与手的部位或活动有关的事物。

The ancient character is like a five-fingered hand in ancient Chinese. When used as a radical, it can be put on the right of or underneath other characters. When put on the left, it appears as "扌", call "the hand radical", indicating thing related to the hand.

手	shǒu	（名） hand
手机	shǒujī	（名） mobile phone
二手	èrshǒu	（名） second-hand

75

看 Look

手搭凉棚向前方看。
Putting hands before the forehead.

看 　 kàn 　 (名) 　 look
看见 　 kàn jiàn 　 　 catch sight of; see
好看 　 hǎokàn 　 (形) 　 good-looking

拿 　 ná 　 (动) 　 hold; take

把 　 bǎ 　 (介) 　 used when the object is the receiver of the action of the ensuring verb
把 　 bǎ 　 (量) 　 a measure word for a tool with a handle and sth. can be picked up with one hand

抱 　 bào 　 (动) 　 hold or carry in the arm

打	打 dǎ	(动)	beat
掉	掉 diào	(动)	fall; drop; lose
	掉头 diào tóu		turn round
挂	挂 guà	(动)	hang; put up
	挂号 guà hào		register
换	换 huàn	(动)	exchange; change
	交换 jiāohuàn	(动)	exchange
接	接 jiē	(动)	join; meet; accept
拉	拉 lā	(动)	pull

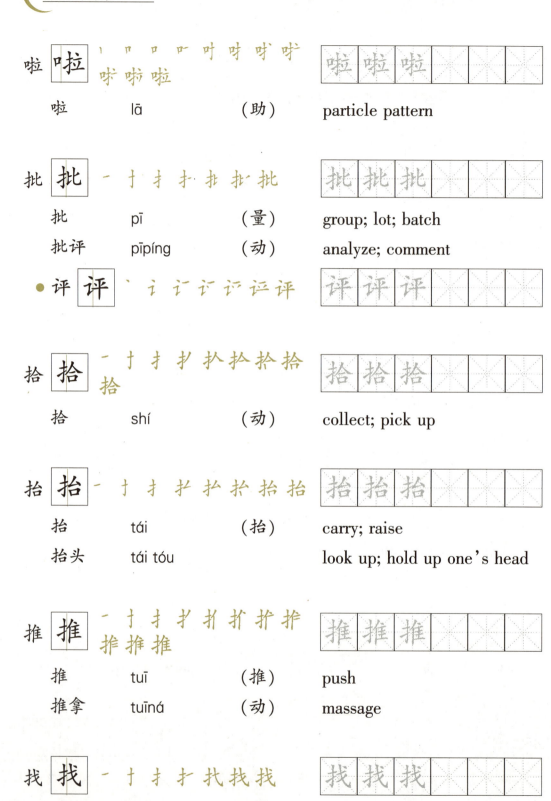

啦	lā	（助）	particle pattern
批	pī	（量）	group; lot; batch
批评	pīpíng	（动）	analyze; comment
评	píng		
拾	shí	（动）	collect; pick up
抬	tái	（抬）	carry; raise
抬头	tái tóu		look up; hold up one's head
推	tuī	（推）	push
推拿	tuīná	（动）	massage
找	zhǎo	（动）	look for; find out

| 手指 | shǒuzhǐ | (名) | finger |
| 指 | zhǐ | (动) | point to |

练习
Exercises

一、连连看(Link the characters and the *Pinyin*)：

抬头　　　　　　diào tóu
手机　　　　　　shǒujī
掉头　　　　　　shǒuzhǐ
手指　　　　　　tái tóu

二、按照笔画由少到多排列下面的汉字(Re-match the characters according to their amount of strokes)

手　换　推　找　挂　打

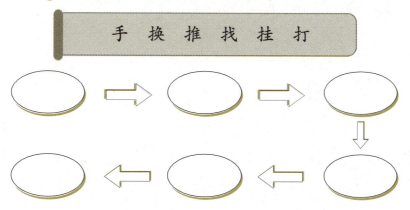

79

三、用所给汉字组成词语(Form words with the given characters)：

看：_____ _____

手：_____ _____

头：_____ _____

找：_____ _____

四、请指出下列每组汉字中共有的部件（Please write down the common component in the following characters）：

吧 把：_____   推 谁：_____

拿 拾：_____   抬 始：_____

五、选词填空(Fill in the blanks with the appropriate characters or words)：

1. _____ 姐姐毕业了，她要 _____ 工作。

    a. 抓   b. 找   c. 我

2. 小男孩 _____ 了一个书包。

    a. 抬   b. 拾

3. 哥哥写得 _____ 我好。

    a. 批   b. 毕   c. 比

第二课 又
Lesson 2 The 又 Radical

汉字和汉语词汇
Chinese Characters and Words

又 Again

　　古文字形象一只伸出来的右手。用作偏旁，"又"在一些字中仍可表示与手的动作有关的事物。

　　在汉字简化的过程中，由于被用来替代一些汉字中笔画较多的偏旁，"又"有时只是一个不表示任何意义的书写符号。

　　"又"后来借作副词，表示重复。

　　The ancient character is like a held-out right hand. when used as a radical, "又" still retains reference to things connected with the hand.

　　During the course of simplifying the Chinese characters, "又" was used to replace some components with many strokes, and thus sometimes it is only a written symbol that has no meanings.

　　Later, "又" became an adverb indicating repetition.

又　　　　yòu　　　　（副）　　

again; as well as

双

| 双 | shuāng | (形、量) | double; both; a pair of |
| 双方 | shuāngfāng | (名) | both sides |

支

| 支 | zhī | (量) | a measure word for long, thin, inflexible objects |

反

| 反 | fǎn | (动、形) | turn over; be against; inside out |
| 反面 | fǎnmiàn | (名) | reverse side; back |

友 Friend

古文字形象两只右手，表示互相帮助的两个人。

The Share of the ancient character looks like two right hands in ancient Chinese, indicating two people helping each other.

友 一 ナ 方 友

| 朋友 | péngyou | （名） | friend |
| 友好 | yǒuhǎo | （形） | friendly; nice |

● 朋 朋　ノ 丿 月 月 刖 朋 朋 朋

发 发　一 丷 方 发 发

发	fā	（动）	send
出发	chūfā	（动）	set out
头发	tóufa	（名）	hair

● 出 出　一 凵 屮 出 出

左 左　一 ナ 广 才 左

| 左 | zuǒ | （名） | left |

右 右　一 ナ 才 右 右

| 右 | yòu | （名） | right |
| 左右 | zuǒyòu | （名） | about |

变 变　一 亠 广 亣 亦 峦 变

变	biàn	（动）	change; become
变化	biànhuà	（动）	change; vary
变心	biàn xīn		a change of heart

新编汉字津梁

观 | 观 | ㄱ 又 㚈 观 观 观
观看　　guānkàn　　（动）　　look at; watch
参观　　cānguān　　（动）　　look around; visit

● 参 | 参 | ㄥ ㄙ 亠 牟 矣 矣 参 参

众 Many

古文字形象三个人，也就是许多人在太阳下干活儿的情景。繁体字写作"眾"，简化为"众"。

The shape of the ancient character looks like three persons, indicating the scene of many people working in the sun. The classical version is "眾", the simplified version is "众".

众 | 众 | ノ 人 亽 夵 众 众
观众　　guānzhòng　　（名）　　audience

欢 | 欢 | ㄱ 又 㚈 欢 欢 欢
喜欢　　xǐhuan　　（动）　　be fond of; enjoy

● 喜 | 喜 | 一 十 士 吉 吉 吉 吉 喜 壴 喜 喜 喜

84

难 | 难 | フ 又 ヌ 对 对 对 坏 | 难 难
| 难 | nán | （形） | difficult; hard
| 难看 | nánkàn | （形） | ugly

取 Take

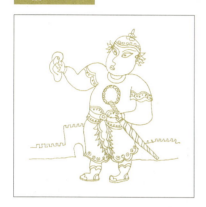

用右手割取俘虏的左耳,这是古代记录战功的方法。

It was a way to record one's merits in a war to cut the captive's left ear off with the right hand.

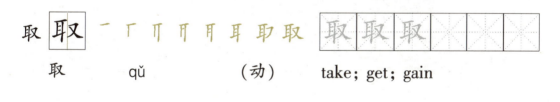

取 | 取 | 一 厂 ㄏ 戸 耳 耳 取 取 | 取 取 取
| 取 | qǔ | （动） | take; get; gain

最 | 最 |  | 最 最 最
| 最 | zuì | （副） | most
| 最好 | zuìhǎo | （副） | best; first-rate

报 | 报 | 一 十 扌 扌 扩 护 报 报 | 报 报 报
| 报 | bào | （名） | newspaper
| 日报 | rìbào | （名） | daily

练习
Exercises

一、连连看(Link the characters and the *Pinyin*)：

二、按照笔画由少到多排列下面的汉字(Re-match the characters according to their amount of strokes)

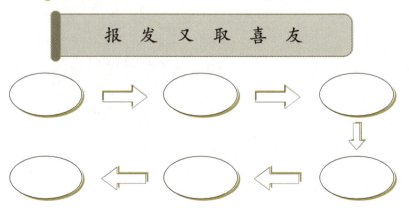

三、用所给汉字组成词语(Form words with the given characters)：

友：_____ _____

变：_____ _____

观：_____ _____

看：_____ _____

四、请指出下列每组汉字中共有的部件（Please write down the common component in the following characters）：

欢　歌：_____　　　友　左：_____

章　意：_____　　　发　支：_____

五、选择填空(Fill in the blanks with the appropriate characters or words)：

1. 他是我最好的朋_____。

　　a. 支　　b. 右　　c. 友　　d. 反

2. 她是_____？

　　a. 难　　b. 谁　　c. 推

3. 我喜_____看报。

　　a. 双　　b. 欢　　c. 观

4. 妹妹的头_____真好看。

　　a. 友　　b. 左　　c. 右　　d. 发

第三课　寸和爪
Lesson 3　The 寸 and 爪 Radical

汉字和汉语词汇
Chinese Characters and Words

寸　The 寸 Radical

古文字形象在手下加一个指事性符号，指出离手掌一寸动脉所在的位置。用作偏旁，多写在字的右边或下边，可表示与手的动作有关的事物。

The ancient character is like that a symbol was put under the hand, pointing at the artery one inch away from the hand. It is usually put on the right of or underneath other characters to indicate things related to the hand.

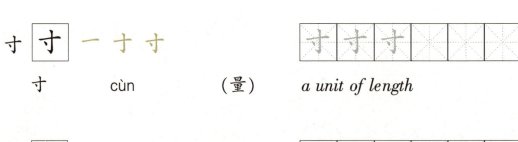

寸　寸　一 十 寸　　　cùn　　（量）　a unit of length

付　付　ノ 亻 亻 付 付　　fù　　（动）　hand over to; pay

付出　　fùchū　　　　（动）　　pay out

导　ㄱ ㅋ 巳 巴 导 导　导 导 导
　向导　　xiàngdǎo　　（名）　　guide
　领导　　lǐngdǎo　　（动、名）　lead; leader

· 向　ノ 亻 门 向 向 向　向 向 向

· 领　ノ ㇀ ㇇ 今 令 令 令 钅 钅 领 领 领　领 领 领

讨　丶 讠 讠 讨 讨　讨 讨 讨
　讨　　tǎo　　　　（动）　　court; beg for
　讨论　　tǎolùn　　　（动）　　discuss

对　ㄱ 又 又 对 对　对 对 对
　对　　duì　　　　（形）　　right; corrected
　反对　　fǎnduì　　　（动）　　oppose; argue against

傅　ノ 亻 亻 亻 伊 伊 伊 伸 伸 傅 傅　傅 傅 傅
　师傅　　shīfu　　　　（名）　　teacher; master

爪 Hand

古文字形象一只在抓拿东西的手，用作偏旁，也可写在字的上边，写作"爫"，叫作爪（zhuǎ）字头。

The ancient character is like a hand in a grabbing gesture. As a component it can also be put on top, written as "爫" called "the head of hand".

爪	爪	丿 厂 爪 爪		
	爪子	zhuǎzi	（名）	claw

抓	抓	一 扌 扌 扩 扩 抓 抓		
	抓	zhuā	（动）	grasp; scratch

爬	爬	丿 厂 爪 爪 爬 爬 爬		
	爬	pá	（动）	crawl; climb
	爬山	pá shān		climb a hill

• | 山 | 山 | 丨 山 山 | | |
| --- | --- | --- | --- | --- |

爱	爱	一 丷 丷 爫 爫 爫 爫 爫 爱 爱		
	爱	ài	（动）	love
	可爱	kě'ài	（形）	lovable; lovely; cute

受 受 ㄧ ㄈ ㄈ ㄈ ㄸ ㄸ 吗 受 受　受 受 受

接受	jiēshòu	（动）	accept
难受	nánshòu	（形）	feel uncomfortable
受不了	shòubuliǎo		cannot stand
受得了	shòudeliǎo		can stand

• 得 得 ノ ノ ィ 彳 彳 彳 彳 彳 彳 得 得　得 得 得

当 当 ⎯ ⎯ ⎯ 当 当 当　当 当 当

当	dāng	（动、介）	serve as；when
应当	yīngdāng	（助动）	should
上当	shàng dàng		take in

争 争 ノ ク ク 乌 乌 争　争 争 争

| 争取 | zhēngqǔ | （动） | try for |
| 争论 | zhēnglùn | （动） | dispute |

妻 Wife

一个坐着的女子用手梳理头发，古文字形象将为人妻的女子改变自己的发型，是"妻子"的意思。

The image of a sitting woman making her hair up in ancient Chinese indicates that a woman to be married changes her hairstyle, and this image means a wife.

| 妻子 | qīzi | （名） | wife |
| 夫妻 | fūqī | （名） | husband and wife |

| 一共 | yígòng | （形） | common；share；altogether |
| 公共 | gōnggòng | （形） | public; common; communal |

| 举 | jǔ | （动） | lift；raise |

练习
Exercises

一、连连看(Link the characters and the *Pinyin*)：

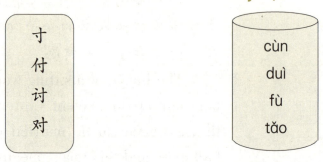

二、按照笔画由少到多排列下面的汉字(Re-match the characters according to their amount of strokes)：

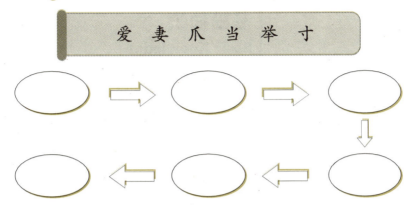

三、用所给汉字组成词语(Form words with the given characters)：

论：_____ _____

争：_____ _____

当：_____ _____

妻：_____ _____

四、请指出下列每组汉字中共有的部件 (Please write down the common component in the following characters)：

颜 领：_____　　讨 论：_____

傅 得：_____　　爬 把：_____

五、选词填空(Fill in the blanks with the appropriate words)：

1. 我们要_____山。
　　a. 抓　　b. 爪　　c. 爬

2. 他_____上了她。
　　a. 受　　b. 爱

3. 他和他爸爸_____论工作。
　　a. 对　　b. 付　　c. 讨

基础知识
Basic Knowledge

汉字的书写规律·竖钩的变化
Conventions of Writing Chinese Characters·
Variations of the Vertical Stroke Ending with a Rising Hook

竖钩的下面还有笔画或部件时,竖钩写作竖。例如:

When there are more stroked or radicals under the vertical stroke ending with a rising hook , it should be written as a vertical, e.g.

小—少:小 + 丿   可—哥:可 + 可

含有竖钩的偏旁写在字的左上方(或左边)时,竖钩写作撇。例如:

When a radical with a vertical stroke ending with a rising hook is on the upper-left hand of a character, the vertical stroke with a rising hook should be written as a left downward stroke, e.g.

手—看:手 + 目

简繁对照
Comparison of Simplified Characters and Classical Characters

评—評	机—機	双—雙	发—發、髮	变—變
参—參	观—觀	众—衆	欢—歡	难—難
报—報	领—領	导—導	讨—討	对—對
爱—愛	当—當	举—舉		

第五单元　身心

Unit 5 Body and Heart

第一课　身体和病痛
Lesson 1　Body and Sick

汉字和汉语词汇
Chinese Characters and Words

身 Body

古文字形象大腹便便的男子的侧面，是一个有地位的受人尊敬的人的形象。这也就是我们今天所说的"身份"的"身"。也有学者认为古文字形象一个怀有身孕的妇女形象。

现代汉字中，"身"可以独立成字，也可用作偏旁，写在字的左边或中间，可表示与身体有关的事物。

The ancient character is like the silhouette of a man with a big belly, who is respected for high social status. This is the "身" as in "status" we talk of today. Some scholars, though, maintain that it's the image of a pregnant woman in ancient Chinese.

In modern Chinese, "身" can be used alone as a character; it can also be used as a radical, put on the left or in the middle, to mean things related with the body.

| 身 | 身 | ㇒ ㇇ 丨 冂 白 自 身 身 | 身 身 身 | | | |

身	shēn	（名、量）	body
身上	shēnshang	（名）	on one's body; have sth. with one
身高	shēngāo	（名）	stature; height of a person
身体	shēntǐ	（名）	body; health

● 高 高 丶 亠 广 ㇄ 古 古 高 高 高 高

● 体 体 ㇒ 亻 亻 什 仕 休 体

| 躲 | 躲 | ㇒ ㇇ 丨 冂 白 自 身 身 躯 躯 躯 躲 躲 |

| 躲 | duǒ | （动） | go into hiding; avoid; dodge |

| 躺 | 躺 | ㇒ ㇇ 丨 冂 白 自 身 身 躺 躺 躺 躺 躺 躺 躺 |

| 躺 | tǎng | （动） | to lie (down) |

| 射 | 射 | ㇒ ㇇ 丨 冂 白 自 身 身 射 射 |

| 射门 | shè mén | | shoot |

| 谢 | 谢 | 丶 亠 讠 讠 讠 讠 讠 讠 谢 谢 谢 谢 |

| 谢谢 | xièxie | （动） | to thank |

疒 The "疒" radical

古代字形象大汗淋漓的人躺在床上，是"生病"的意思。用作偏旁，写作"疒"(nè)，叫病字旁。

The ancient character looks like a sick person in bed sweltering, meaning "sick". The character later was turned into a part, called "the sickness radical".

病　丶一广广广疒疒病病病

病	bìng	（名、动）	sickness; to be sick
病人	bìngrén	（名）	patient
病房	bìngfáng	（名）	sickroom; ward
看病	kàn bìng		to see a doctor
生病	shēng bìng		to contract a disease

房　丶一广户户房房

疼　丶一广广广广疒疼疼

痛　丶一广广广广疒疒病病痛痛

| 疼 | téng | （形、动） | ache; pain |
| 头疼 | tóuténg | （动、形） | headache |

疼痛　téngtòng　　　（动）　　　ache; be in pain

瘦　｜瘦｜　丶 亠 广 广 疒 疒 疒 疒 疒 疒 疒 痩 痩 瘦

瘦　　shòu　　　　（形）　　　thin; skinny
瘦小　shòuxiǎo　　（形）　　　thin and small

疯　｜疯｜　丶 亠 广 广 疒 疒 疘 疯 疯

疯　　fēng　　　　（形）　　　mad; insane; crazy
疯子　fēngzi　　　（名）　　　madman; lunatic

癌　｜癌｜　丶 亠 广 广 疒 疒 疒 疒 疒 痞 痞 瘟 癌 癌 癌

癌　　ái　　　　　（名）　　　cancer

练习
Exercises

一、请指出下列形符的名称和意义 (Please link the name and meaning of the given radical):

身　　病字旁

疒　　身字旁

二、按照笔画由少到多排列下面的汉字（Re-match the characters according to their amount of strokes）

躺　病　瘦　疯　体　谢

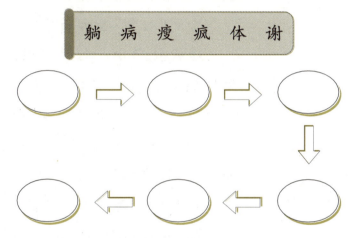

三、请指出下列每组汉字中共有的部件（Please write down the common component in the following characters）：

躺　躲：_____　　　病　疼：_____

射　付：_____　　　高　京：_____

四、用所给汉字组成词语（Form words with the given characters）：

身：_____　　_____

病：_____　　_____

疼：_____　　_____

第二课　心（一）
Lesson 2　Heart（Ⅰ）

汉字和汉语词汇
Chinese Characters and Words

心　The Heart Radical

古文"心"是心脏的象形。

现代汉字中，"心"可以独立成字。用作偏旁时可写在字的下边，作"心"，叫心字底（dǐ）；也可写在字的左边，作"忄"，叫竖（shù）心旁；可写在字的下边，还可写作"㣺"，叫竖心底。都可表示与人的心理活动有关的事物。

The ancient character "心" takes the shape of heart.

In modern Chinese, 心 can be used as an independent character. As a radical, it can be put underneath other characters as "心" and it's called the "xin zi di"; it can also be put on the left as "忄", called "shu xin pang", when put at the bottom, the radical can also be written as "㣺", called "shu xin di". It means things that are connected with a person's psychology.

第五单元 身心

心

心	xīn	（名）	heart
小心	xiǎoxīn	（形、动）	to be careful
担心	dān xīn		angst; take thought for
放心	fàng xīn		disburden; reassurance
关心	guānxīn	（动）	to show solicitude for
耐心	nàixīn	（形、名）	patient; patience

• 担

放

关

• 耐

必

| 必须 | bìxū | （助动、动） | must |

• 须

急

| 急 | jí | （形） | worried; anxious |
| 着急 | zháojí | （形） | to worry about; to be worried about |

| 念 | niàn | （动） | to read |
| 念书 | niàn shū | | to read (a book) |

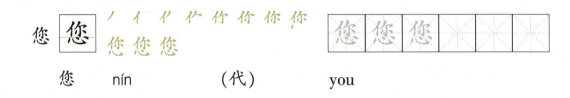

您　nín　　　（代）　　you

态度　tàidu　　（名）　　attitude

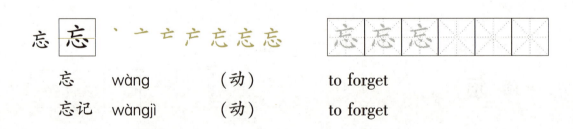

| 忘 | wàng | （动） | to forget |
| 忘记 | wàngjì | （动） | to forget |

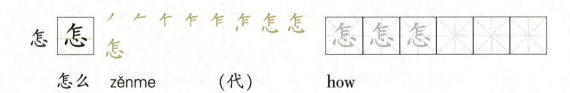

怎么　zěnme　　（代）　　how

意

意见	yìjiàn	（名）	grouch
同意	tóngyì	（动）	to agree
生意	shēngyi	（名）	business
主意	zhǔyi	（名）	idea

- 同 丨 冂 冂 同 同 同

- 主 丶 亠 二 宇 主

思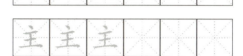

思念	sīniàn	（动）	miss; have in mind
意思	yìsi	（名）	meaning
不好意思	bù hǎoyìsi		to be shy

练习
Exercises

一、连连看(Link the characters and the *Pinyin*)：

二、按照笔画由少到多排列下面的汉字(Re-match the characters according to their amount of strokes)

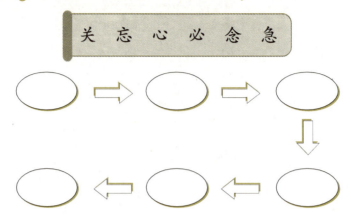

关 忘 心 必 念 急

三、用所给汉字组成词语(Form words with the given characters)：

心：_____ _____

意：_____ _____

思：_____ _____

四、请指出下列每组汉字中共有的部件 (Please write down the common component in the following characters)：

着 差：_____   作 怎：_____

章 意：_____   变 恋：_____

五、选词填空(Fill in the blanks with the appropriate words)：

1. 他喜欢_____着看书。

　a. 谢　　b. 躺　　c. 射

2. 我的哥哥_____爱了。

　a. 恋　　b. 变

3. A：你_____了？

　B：我头疼。

　a. 怎么　　b. 什么

第三课 心（二）
Lesson 3　Heart（Ⅱ）

汉字和汉语词汇
Chinese Characters and Words

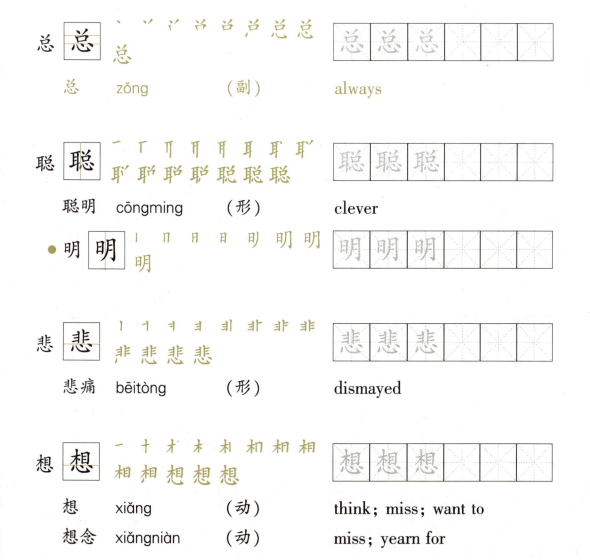

总　zǒng　（副）　always

聪明　cōngming　（形）　clever

明

悲痛　bēitòng　（形）　dismayed

想　xiǎng　（动）　think; miss; want to
想念　xiǎngniàn　（动）　miss; yearn for

感　感　一厂厂厂厂后后咸咸
　　　　咸咸感感感

感谢　gǎnxiè　（动）　　　to thank
感到　gǎndào　（动）　　　find; taste
感觉　gǎnjué　（动、名）　to feel; feeling
感冒　gǎnmào　（动、名）　to catch a cold

• 到　到　一 工 云 至 至 至 到
　　　　 到

• 冒　冒　丨 冂 冂 曰 冐 冒 冒
　　　　 冒 冒

恋　恋　、一 亠 亣 亦 亦 恋
　　　　恋 恋

恋爱　liàn'ài　（动、名）　to love; the state of being in love

愿　愿　一 厂 厂 厂 庐 庐 庐 原
　　　　原 原 原 愿 愿 愿

愿意　yuànyì　（助动、动）　care for; with pleasure; would like to

回 Return

古文字形象水流、河道回环往复的样子。

The ancient character is like flowing water, and circling of rivers.

第五单元 身心

忆　丶 丶 忄 忆

| 回忆 | huíyì | （动、名） | to remember; memory |
| 记忆 | jìyì | （动、名） | memory |

● 回　丨 冂 冂 回 回 回

快　丶 丶 忄 忄 快 快

愉　丶 丶 忄 忄 忄 忄 忄 愉 愉 愉 愉 愉

快	kuài	（形）	quick; fast
快乐	kuàilè	（形）	happy
痛快	tòngkuai	（形）	to one's heart's content
愉快	yúkuài	（形）	pleasure; delight

● 乐　丿 二 于 乐 乐

慢　丶 丶 忄 忄 忄 忄 忄 悒 悒 悒 悒 慢 慢

| 慢 | màn | （形） | slow |

惯　丶 丶 忄 忄 忄 忄 忄 惯 惯 惯 惯

| 惯 | guàn | （动） | spoil |
| 习惯 | xíguàn | （名、动） | habit; be used to |

练习
Exercises

一、按照笔画由少到多排列下面的汉字（Re-match the characters according to their amount of strokes）

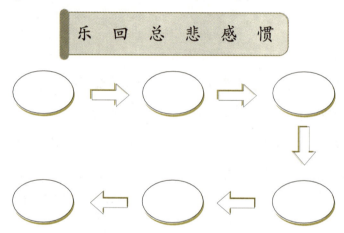

二、用所给汉字组成词语（Form words with the given characters）：

记：_____ _____ _____

快：_____ _____ _____

感：_____ _____ _____

三、请指出下列每组汉字中共有的部件（Please write down the common component in the following characters）：

忆 亿：_____   排 悲：_____

职 聪：_____   变 恋：_____

四、选词填空(Fill in the blanks with the appropriate words)：

1. 来中国以后,她很_____父母。

   a. 思   b. 想   c. 念

2. 这几天天气不好,小心不要_____冒了。

   a. 喊   b. 感

3. 他的女儿很_____明。

   a. 聪   b. 总

第四课　心（三）
Lesson 4　Heart（Ⅲ）

汉字和汉语词汇
Chinese Characters and Words

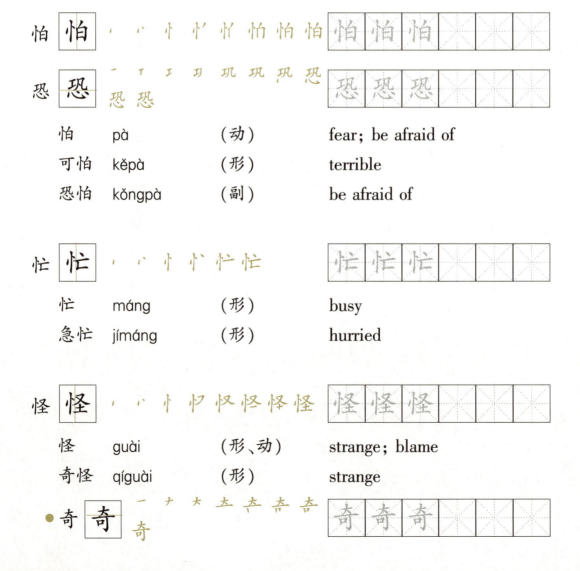

怕	pà	（动）	fear; be afraid of
可怕	kěpà	（形）	terrible
恐怕	kǒngpà	（副）	be afraid of

| 忙 | máng | （形） | busy |
| 急忙 | jímáng | （形） | hurried |

| 怪 | guài | （形、动） | strange; blame |
| 奇怪 | qíguài | （形） | strange |

第五单元 身心

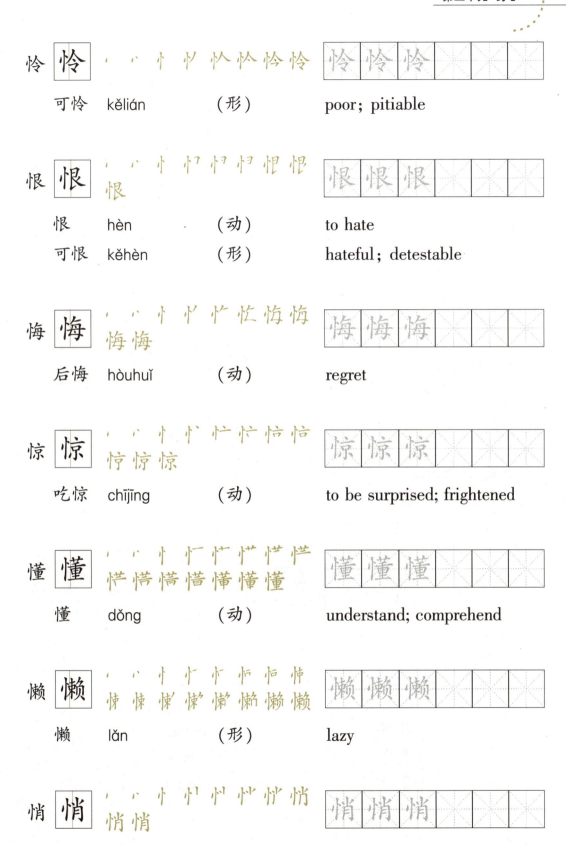

可怜　kělián　（形）　poor; pitiable

恨　hèn　（动）　to hate
可恨　kěhèn　（形）　hateful; detestable

后悔　hòuhuǐ　（动）　regret

吃惊　chījīng　（动）　to be surprised; frightened

懂　dǒng　（动）　understand; comprehend

懒　lǎn　（形）　lazy

五

113

悄悄　qiāoqiāo　　　（副）　　　quietly

愤　愤　丶 丷 忄 忄 忄 忄 忄 忄 愤 愤 愤 愤

怒　怒　乙 女 女 如 奴 奴 怒 怒 怒

愤怒　fènnù　　　（形）　　　anger; wrath; fury; indignation

小　The "小" Radical

• 羡　羡　丶 丷 斗 羊 羊 羊 羊 羊 羊 羊 羡

慕　慕　一 十 艹 艹 苎 苎 苜 莒 莫 莫 莫 慕 慕 慕

羡慕　xiànmù　　　（动）　　　admire

练习
Exercises

一、连连看(Link the characters and the *Pinyin*)：

习惯　　　qíguài
喜欢　　　xǐhuan
奇怪　　　xíguàn

二、按照笔画由少到多排列下面的汉字(Re-match the characters according to their amount of strokes)

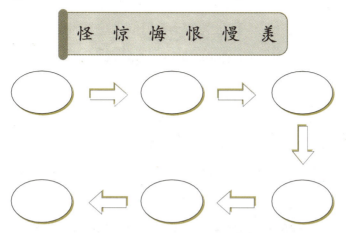

怪 惊 悔 恨 慢 羡

三、用所给汉字组成词语(Form words with the given characters)：

可：_____ _____

怕：_____ _____

四、请指出下列每组汉字中共有的部件 (Please write down the common component in the following characters)：

很 恨：_____   耐 对：_____

快 慢：_____   羡 美：_____

五、选词填空(Fill in the blanks with the appropriate words)：

1. 我太_____了，_____了写信。

   a. 忘   b. 忙

2. 这个词的意思你明_____吗?

   a. 怕   b. 白

3. 车开得太快了，我有点儿_____。

   a. 可怕   b. 恐怕   c. 怕

4. 这个孩子很小就没有了父母，很_____。

   a. 可怜   b. 着急

基础知识
Basic Knowledge

汉字的造字方法·象形
Ways How Characters Were Created·Hieroglyphic Characters

根据客观事物的外在形态来结构汉字形体的方法叫象形。例如：
Hieroglyphic characters are created according to the appearance of objective things. For instance:

① 日 (sun)

② 马 (horse)

③ 心 (heart)

④ 水 (water)

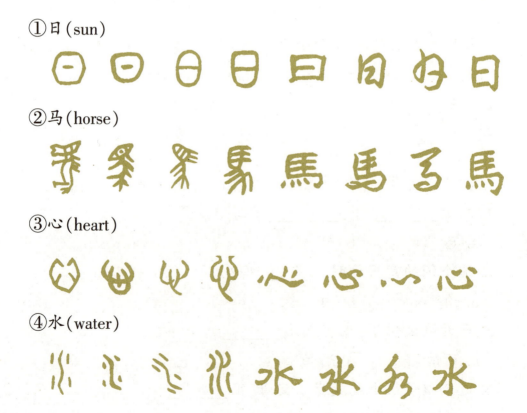

第五单元 身心

⑤车(vehicle)

⑥山(mountain)

⑦不(no)

⑧刀(knife)

简繁对照

Comparison of Simplified Characters and Classical Characters

谢—謝	态—態	总—總	恋—戀
愿—願	聪—聰	忆—憶	怜—憐
惊—驚	惯—慣	疯—瘋	愤—憤
懒—懶	体—體	关—關	义—義
动—動	乐—樂	热—熱	

五

第六单元 足

Unit 6 Foot

第一课 止
Lesson 1 Toes

汉字和汉语词汇
Chinese Characters and Words

止 Toes

古文字形象人的脚趾，后来写成"止"。"止"借作"停止"讲以后，就又造了一个"趾"表示它本来的意义：其中的"足"表示人的下肢器官。"止"既表达意义，又表示字的声音。

"止"在现代汉字中可用作偏旁，可写成"止"、"止"或"足"，但并不一定都与行走有关。

The ancient character is like one's toes in ancient Chinese. Later it was written as "止". When "止" was corrupted to mean "stop" later, "趾" was created to replace it to mean the old thing. "足" means organs in the lower part of the body, and "止" suggests both meaning and pronunciation.

In modern Chinese characters, when used as a radical, "止" has the following three versions "止", "止" and "足".

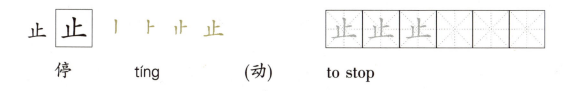

止　停　tíng　（动）　to stop

停止　　tíngzhǐ　　（动）　　to stop

停 | ノ 亻 亻 广 广 佇 佇 佇 佇 停

正 Right

古文字形上边表示有许多人居住的城邑，下象护卫城邑的人的脚。

The upper part of "正" means a city with dwellers, and the lower parts means the feet of the dwellers.

正 | 一 T F 正 正

真正　　zhēnzhèng　　（形）　　real; true; genuine
正好　　zhènghǎo　　（副）　　just right

歪 | 一 丁 兀 不 不 不 否 歪 歪

歪　　wāi　　（形）　　oblique

些 | 一 ト 止 止 此 此 些

一些　　yìxiē　　（代）　　some
好些　　hǎoxiē　　（形）　　quite a lot; quite a few

步 Step

左右两脚各向前迈一次为一步,所以古文字形合"止(左脚)"和"少(右脚)"为步。

The forward movement of the left and the right foot combined is a step. So the combination of "止 (left foot)" and "少(右脚)"means a step.

步	bù	（名）	step

是	shì	（动）	to be
可是	kěshì	（连）	but
要是	yàoshì	（连）	if
只是	zhǐshì	（副、连）	only

题	tí	（名）	title
题目	tímù	（名）	title; name
问题	wèntí	（名）	question

提 | 提 | 一 十 扌 扌 扣 捍 捍 捍 捍 捍 提 提 | 提 提 提

| 提 | tí | （动） | to lift; to carry |
| 提包 | tíbāo | （名） | handbag |

先 First

上"止"下"儿（人）"，古文字形用"止"在"人"前表示先行的意思。

The combination of "止" on top and "儿（人）"at the bottom means "first".

先 | 先 | ノ 广 ᅩ 生 失 先 | 先 先 先

| 先 | xiān | （副） | first |
| 先生 | xiānsheng | （名） | mister |

走 Walk

古文字形上边象人奔跑时摆动双臂，迈着大步的形象；下加"止"，突出了人在跑动的意味，所以古文"走"是"奔跑"的意思。

The ancient character looks like a person in strides, swinging arms; "止"is added to this highlight the sense of "running". So "走"in ancient Chinese means to run.

第六单元 足

走 | 走 | 一 十 土 キ キ 走 走 | 走 走 走
走 zǒu （动） to go; to walk

起 | 起 | 一 十 土 キ キ 走 走 走 起 起 | 起 起 起
起 qǐ （动） to get up
起床 qǐ chuáng to get up
一起 yìqǐ （副） together
对不起 duìbuqǐ sorry

• 床 | 床 | 丶 一 广 广 庁 床 床 | 床 床 床

趣 | 趣 | 一 十 土 キ キ 走 走 走 赵 赵 赵 赵 赵 趣 趣 | 趣 趣 趣
兴趣 xìngqù （名） interest; hobby
感兴趣 gǎn xìngqù to be interest in

• 兴 | 兴 | 丶 丶 丷 ⺍ 兴 兴 | 兴 兴 兴

六

练习
Exercises

一、按照笔画由少到多排列下面的汉字(Re-match the characters according to their amount of strokes)

125

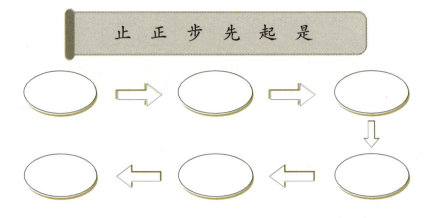

止 正 步 先 起 是

二、用所给汉字组成词语(Form words with the given characters)：

正：_____ _____

是：_____ _____

起：_____ _____

趣：_____ _____

三、请指出下列每组汉字中共有的部件 (Please write down the common component in the following characters)：

丢 摆：_____   起 记：_____

停 京：_____   提 抓：_____

四、选词填空(Fill in the blanks with the appropriate words)：

1. 我买了一个 _____ 包。

   a. 提   b. 题   c. 趣

2. 哥哥每天早上去 _____ 步。

   a. 包   b. 抱   c. 跑

3. 我学了一 _____ 汉字。

   a. 止   b. 正   c. 歪   d. 些

第二课 辶
Lesson 2　The 辶 Radical

汉字的派生笔画
Derivative Strokes of Chinese Characters

横折折撇 héngzhézhépiě

汉字和汉语词汇
Chinese Characters and Words

辶 The 辶 Radical

　　古文字形象人的脚在道路上行走，写作"辵 (chuò)"。
　　现在已经不用单独的"辵"。字形用作偏旁，写作"辶"，因其形体与"之"相似，故称为"走之儿"或"走之旁"，多表示与道路、行走有关的事物。

The shape of the ancient character is like one's feet walking on the road.

"辵" does not exist in modern Chinese characters as an independent character. It is used as a radical, written as"辶", and similar to "之". It means things related to road or walking.

| 这 | 这 | 丶 亠 亇 文 这 这 这 | | 这 这 这 | | | | |

	这	zhè	(代)	this
	这个	zhège	(代)	this
	这儿	zhèr	(代)	here
	这么	zhème	(代)	so
	这些	zhèxiē	(代)	these

| 边 | 边 | フ 力 力 边 边 | | 边 边 边 | | | | |

	北边	běibian	(名)	north
	后边	hòubian	(名)	back
	上边	shàngbian	(名)	above
	下边	xiàbian	(名)	beneath
	右边	yòubian	(名)	right
	左边	zuǒbian	(名)	left
	这边	zhèbiān	(名)	over here
	旁边	pángbiān	(名)	at one's side

• 旁 旁 丶 亠 亠 产 产 产 产 产 旁 旁

| 过 | 过 | 一 寸 寸 过 过 | | 过 过 过 | | | | |

	过	guò	(动、助)	to pass; to have done
	不过	búguò	(连)	but
	难过	nánguò	(动、形)	sad; to feel sad

还 还 一 𠂇 才 不 不 还 还

还	hái	（副）	and; but also
还是	háishì	（副、连）	may as well
还	huán	（动）	to return

进 | 进 | 一 ニ 干 井 讲 进 进

| 进 | jìn | （动） | to enter |
| 进步 | jìnbù | （形、动） | improved; to progress |

近 | 近 | ´ 厂 斤 斤 斤 近 近

| 近 | jìn | （形） | nearby |
| 最近 | zuìjìn | （名） | lately |

远 | 远 | 一 二 亍 元 元 远 远

| 远 | yuǎn | （形） | far |
| 永远 | yǒngyuǎn | （副） | forever |

• 永 | 永 | ` 丁 刁 永 永

送 | 送 | ` ` ` 丷 䒑 关 关 关 送 送

| 送 | sòng | （动） | to see sb. off; to send |

通 | 通 | ` ` ` 冖 丆 甬 甬 甬 甬 通 通

| 通 | tōng | （动、形） | to pass; passable |
| 通过 | tōngguò | （介、动） | to pass; through |

交通　jiāotōng　（名）　traffic
普通　pǔtōng　（形）　ordinary

道　dào　（量）　a measure word for questions. etc

欢迎　huānyíng　（动）　to welcome

古迹　gǔjì　（名）　relics

练习
Exercises

一、连连看 (Link the characters and the *Pinyin*)：

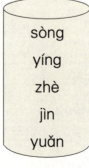

二、按照笔画由少到多排列下面的汉字(Re-match the characters according to their amount of strokes)

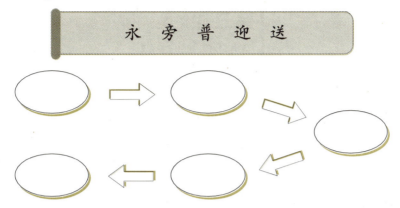

永　旁　普　迎　送

三、用所给汉字组成词语(Form words with the given characters)：

这：_____　_____

边：_____　_____

过：_____　_____

通：_____　_____

四、请指出下列每组汉字中共有的部件 (Please write down the common component in the following characters)：

歪　还：_____　　　听　近：_____

讲　进：_____　　　通　痛：_____

五、选词填空(Fill in the blanks with the appropriate words)：

1. 妹妹最_____总是生病。
   a. 讲　　b. 进　　c. 近

2. 我说_____,你忘了。
   a. 进　　b. 远　　c. 过

3. 这儿的_____很方便。
   a. 普通　b. 交通　c. 通过

第三课 足
Lesson 3　Foot

汉字和汉语词汇
Chinese Characters and Words

足 Foot

古文字形象腿下有"止",即腿脚的样子。

用作偏旁,"足"可写在字下,也可写在字的左边,作"⻊",表示与腿脚的部位、运动或交通有关的事物。

The ancient character looks like to have feet under legs, i.e. legs and feet.

When used as a radical, it can be put at the bottom and on the left, written as "⻊", indicating leg or foot, or things related with movements or transportation.

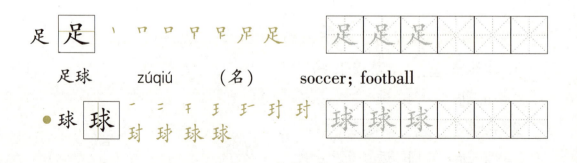

足球　　zúqiú　　（名）　　soccer; football

跟　　　gēn　　　　　　（介、连）　like; and

跑　pǎo　　　（动）　to run
跑步　pǎo bù　　　　to jog

踢　tī　　　（动）　to kick

跳　tiào　　　（动）　to jump

夂 The 夂 radical

人走路时总是先出左脚，所以古文"夂"象是向左，它的本义是从高处下来。用作偏旁，可写在字的上边、下边或左边，称作"折纹儿"。

One usually steps the left foot out when walking, so "夂" in ancient Chinese means "to the left", originally meaning "to come down from a high place". When used as a radical, it can be put either on top, or at the bottom, or on the left, called "the 夂 radical".

| 各 | 各 | ノ ク 夂 冬 各 各 | 各 各 各 |

各　　gè　　（代）　　each

| 路 | 路 | ` ` 口 口 卩 𧾷 𧾷 跂 趵 趵 路 路 | 路 路 路 |

路　　lù　　（名）　　road
路过　　lùguò　　（动）　　to pass by
公路　　gōnglù　　（名）　　road
道路　　dàolù　　（名）　　road; street

| 处 | 处 | ノ ク 夂 处 处 | 处 处 处 |

处处　　chùchù　　（名）　　everywhere
好处　　hǎochu　　（名）　　benefit

| 复 | 复 | ノ 一 个 午 伝 白 甹 复 | 复 复 复 |

复习　　fùxí　　（动）　　to review
复印　　fùyìn　　（动）　　to photocopy

• 印　印　　ノ 匚 F 臼 印

印 印 印

| 夏 | 夏 | 一 丆 丆 丆 百 百 頁 夏 夏 | 夏 夏 夏 |

夏天　　xiàtiān　　（名）　　summer

舞 Dance

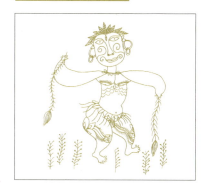

古文字形象双手拿着毛饰舞蹈的形象。

The shape of the ancient character looks like a man dancing with furry things in hand.

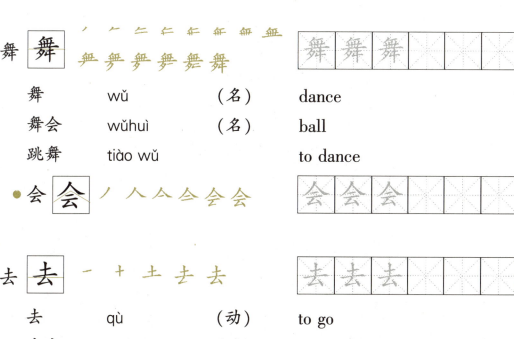

舞	wǔ	(名)	dance
舞会	wǔhuì	(名)	ball
跳舞	tiào wǔ		to dance

● 会 ノ 人 人 会 会 会

去	qù	(动)	to go
出去	chūqu	(动)	to go out
上去	shàngqu	(动)	to go up
下去	xiàqu	(动)	to go down
回去	huíqu	(动)	to go back
过去	guòqu	(动)	to go past
过去	guòqù	(名)	past
进去	jìnqu	(动)	to go in

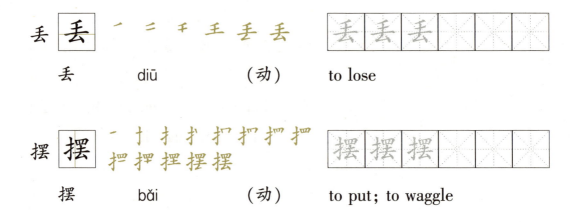

丢　　　diū　　　（动）　　　to lose

摆　　　bǎi　　　（动）　　　to put; to waggle

> 练习
> Exercises

一、连连看 (Link the characters and the *Pinyin*)：

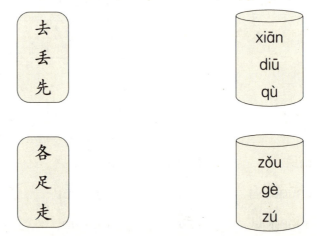

二、按照笔画由少到多排列下面的汉字 (Re-match the characters according to their amount of strokes)

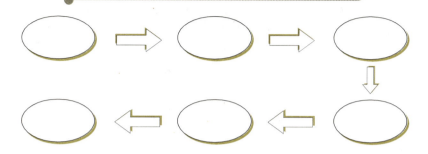

三、用所给汉字组成词语(Form words with the given characters)：

路：_____ _____

复：_____ _____

舞：_____ _____

去：_____ _____

四、选词填空(Fill in the blanks with the appropriate words)：

1. 我 _____ 朋友一起去跳舞。

　　a. 眼　　b. 跟　　c. 很

2. 我的哥哥最喜欢 _____ 足球了。

　　a. 跑　　b. 跳　　c. 踢　　d. 路

3. 这个 _____ 天我和同学去南方。

　　a. 复　　b. 夏

4. 我的书包 _____ 了。

　　a. 去　　b. 丢　　c. 先　　d. 走

基础知识
Basic Knowledge

汉字的造字方法·指事
Ways How Characters Were Created·Self-explanatory Characters

用象征性的符号来表示字的意义的造字方法叫指事。

指事字可分为两种。一种是纯符号的，如短横在上，长横在下表示"上"；反过来长横在上，短横在下表示"下"。另一种是在象形字的基础上加一个指事性符号，如在"木"上加"一"作"末"，表示树的末梢；在"木"下加"一"作"本"，表示树的根。在这里，"一"不是数字的"一"，而仅仅是一个符号。又比如，"刀"加"、"指示着刀刃所在地部位；一个直立的人（大）左右两"、"指示着腋下所在的部位（亦）。这里的"、"都是指事符号。

The way to form a character using symbols to indicate the character's meaning is called "Self-explanatory Characters". There are two types of indication: one is purely symbolic, e.g. a shorter horizontal over a longer means "up", and the opposite means "down"; the other type is to add a symbol to hieroglyphic character, e.g. adding a "一"to "木" means the end of a tree (本). Here, the "一"is not the numeric, but a mere symbol. For instance, a knife （刀）with an additional dot indicates where the blade is. The left and right points in "人" indicates armpits. The dots here are all indication symbol.

① 上 (up)

② 下 (down)

③ 末 (end)

④ 本 (root)

⑤ 刃 (edge of a knife)

⑥ 亦 (also)

简繁对照
Comparison of Simplified Characters and Classical Characters

题—題　　问—問　　兴—興　　这—這
边—邊　　过—過　　还—還　　进—進
远—遠